Table of Contents

North Carolina -Carolina del Norte

South Carolina- Carolina de Sur

Cape Fear- El Cabo De Miedo

North Carolina- Carolina del Norte

South Carolina-Carolina de Sur

North Carolina-Carolina del Norte

North Carolina- Carolina del Norte

North Carolina-Carolina del Norte

Lady and Sons -Damas e Hijos

North Carolina – Carolina del Norte

Tybee Island – Isla Tybee

Tybee Island – Isla Tybee

Tybee Island-Isla Tybee

Tybee Island – Isla Tybee

Tybee Island-Isla Tybee

Tybee Island – Isla Tybee

Tybee Island -Isla Tybee

Tybee Island-Isla Tybee Barrier Islands – La isla de barrea

Sea Islands- Islas del mar Tybee Island – Isla Tybee

Tybee Island – Isla Tybee Savannah River -Rio de Savannah

Savannah River -Rio de Savannah

Savannah River -Rio de Savannah

Savannah River -Rio de Savannah

River Street -Calle del Rio Savannah

River Street – Calle del Rio Savannah

Savannah Historic District – Hito historico de Savannah

River Street -Calle del Rio Savannah

Savannah Historic District – Hito historico de Savannah

River Street -Calle de Rio Savannah

River Street -Calle de Rio Savannah

River Street- Calle de Rio Savannah

Downtown Savannah -El Centro Savannah River Street – Calle de Rio Savannah

River Street- Calle de Rio Savannah

River Street- Calle de Rio Savannah

River Street -Calle de Rio Savannah River Street- Calle de Rio Savannah

River Street – Calle de Rio Savannah

River Street- Calle de Rio Savannah

River Street- Calle de Rio Savannah

Georgia Spanish Moss – Georgia musgo espanol

Florida Spanish Moss- Florida musgo espanol

Virginia Beach Spanish Moss – Playas virginia musgo espanol (Virginia)

Alabama Spanish Moss – Alabama musgo espanol

Mississippi Spanish Moss – Mississippi musgo espanol

South Carolina Spanish Moss – Carolina del Sur musgo espanol

North Carolina -Carolina del Norte – idioma en Ingles

Lowcountry – Pais Bajo-idioma en Ingles

Lowcountry-Paid bajo- idioma en Ingles

Carolina del Sur – Pais bajo

Gullah Red Rice with Smoked Sausages – Arroz rojo Gullah con chorizo ahumado

Rice Production in the 18th Century -Inglesa/English

Rice Production in 18th Century – Inglesa/English

Produccion de arroz el siglo XVIII – lengua espanola

Sea Islands -Islas del Mar

Sea Island Stakeholders – Partes Interesada de las islas del Mar

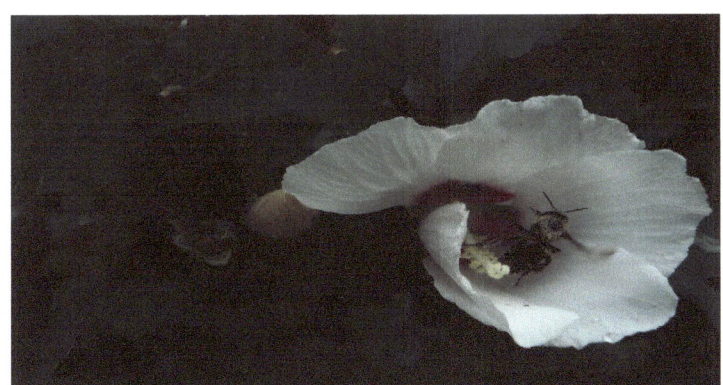

Norte Carolina – Carolina del Norte

Bees are related to southern summertime friends of wasps and ants. Many plants cannot self-fertilize. It is the bee that completes the process of fertilization for the plants and produces the tasty organic honey. The bee enables cross pollination. Bumble Bees and Honeybees can and will sting a person. Call a professional person to remove the beehive on your property. Africanized bees are more aggressive and tend to swarm. If you are chased by a swarm of Africanized bees, run in a zig zag pattern, seek shelter in a house or a car. Jumping in water is a bad idea, the swarm waits for you to come up for air

Bees are also an endangered species due to habitat loss and pesticides Honeybees are not on the endangered Bee species list. People could not exist without bees; bees enable pollination for our food. (Bee Extinction Facts: https://www.scienceabc.com

Las Abejas estan relacionadas con los amigos de sur de Verano de avispas y hormigas. Las personas no pueden existir sin las Abejas, las Abejas polinizan las plantas; nuestra comida.

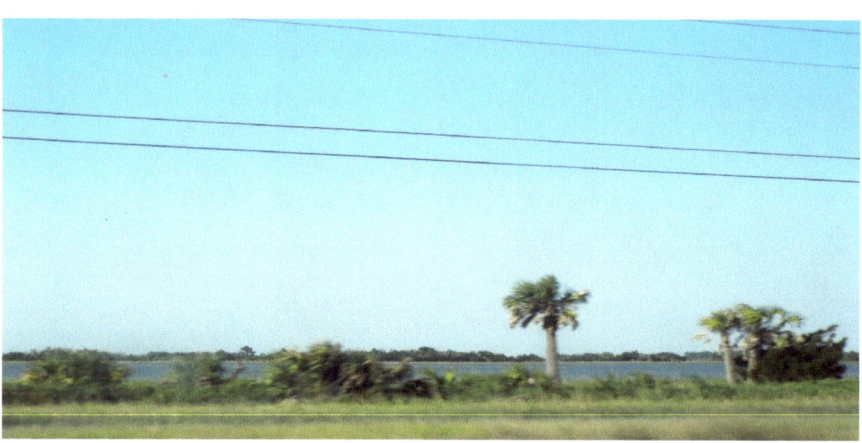

South Carolina -Carolina del Sur

Palm Trees are not trees. Palms are botanically linked with grasses, sedges, lilies, onions, and orchids. Turf grass and corn are more related than an oak tree. Palm Trees are amazing, giant grasses. (Earth Connection-www.the earthconnection.org.)

Las palmeras no son arboles. Las palmeras estian botanicamente vinculadas con pastos, junicas, lirios, cebollas, orquideas. El ceseped y el maiz estan mas relacionados que un roble. Las Palmeras son pastos gigantes increibles.

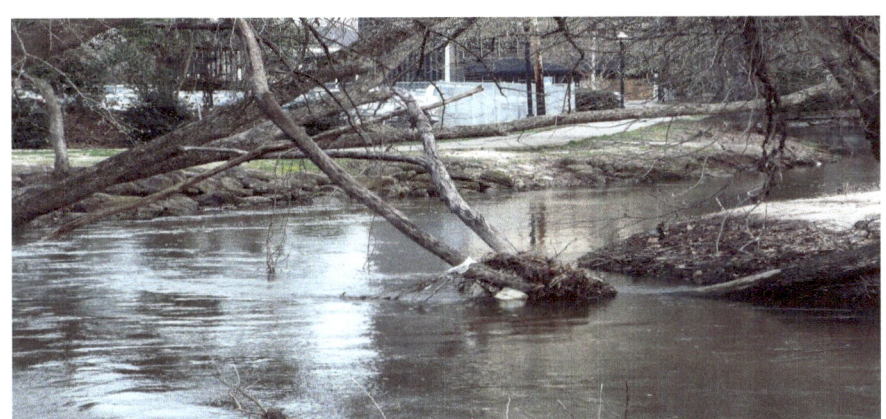

Cape Fear, North Carolina – El Cabo del Miedo, Carolina del Norte

Cape Fear starts in Haywood by the confluence of the Deep and Haw Rivers below Jordan Lake. Cape Fear continues to flow southeast past Lillington, Fayetteville, and Elizabethtown, North Carolina and receives the Black River. (Cape Fear, https://en.m.wikipedia.org/wiki/Cape_Fear_River)

Cape Fear comienza en Haywood por la confluencia de los rios Deep y Haw debajo del lago Jordan. Cape Fear continuia fluyendo hacia el suroeste pasando Lillington, Fayetteville y Elizabethtown, Carolina del Norte, y recibe el Rio Negro

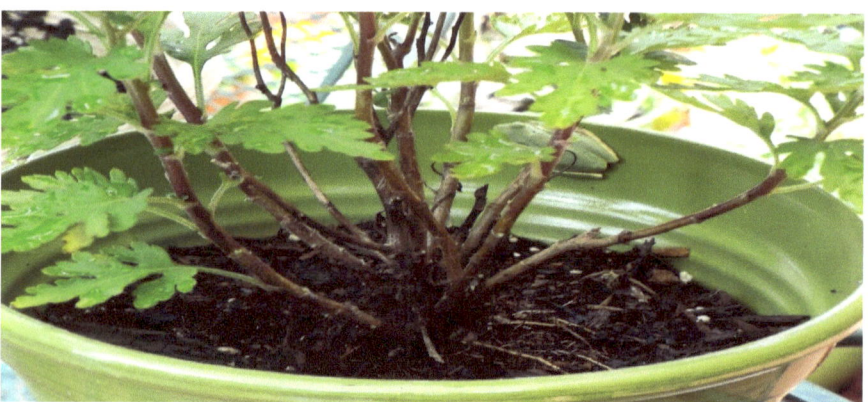

North Carolina – Carolina del Norte

Tree Frog blending with the green foliage and the hue of the flowerpot. The frog appears after 6 days of consistent rainfall in the area. During the day, the treefrogs hide under moist shady area. My deck was a moist wetland after 6 days of consistent rain. The Treefrog is hiding in the right- hand corner of the pot. Did the Treefrog attach eggs to the leaves? The writer does not know. (ncwildlife.org-https://www.ncwildlife.org/Learning/Species/Treefrogs)

Ranas arborea que se mezcia con follaje verde y el tono de la maceta. La rana aparece despues de 6 dias de lluvia constante. Mi cubierta era un humedal humedo. La rana arborease se esconde en la esquina derecho de la maceta. La rana arboricola unia huevos a las hojas. El escritor no lo sabe

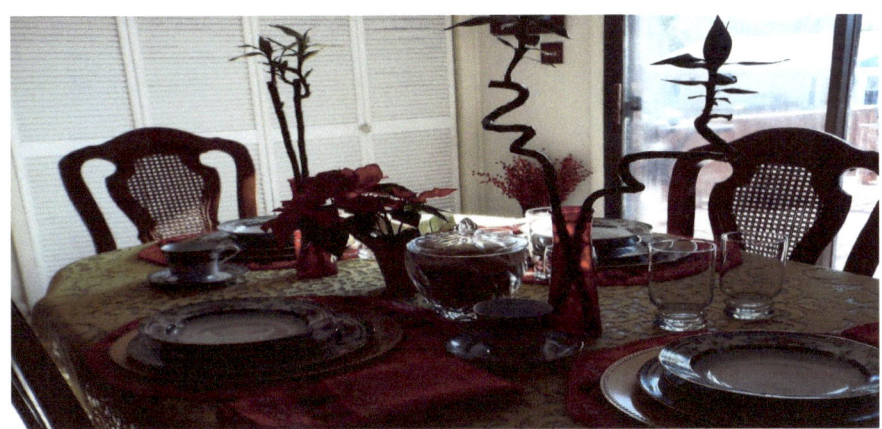

People say, "Beauty is in the eye of the beholder" Beauty is the realization that you are the beholder. This empowers you to find beauty in places where others have not dared to look, inside of yourself, or the table setting in your home.

Salma Hayak

La gente dice:" la belleza esta en el ojo de espectador." La belleza es darse cuenta de que usted es el espectador. Esto le permite encontrar belleza donde otros no se han atrevido a mirar, dentro de usted o en una mesa en su hogar.

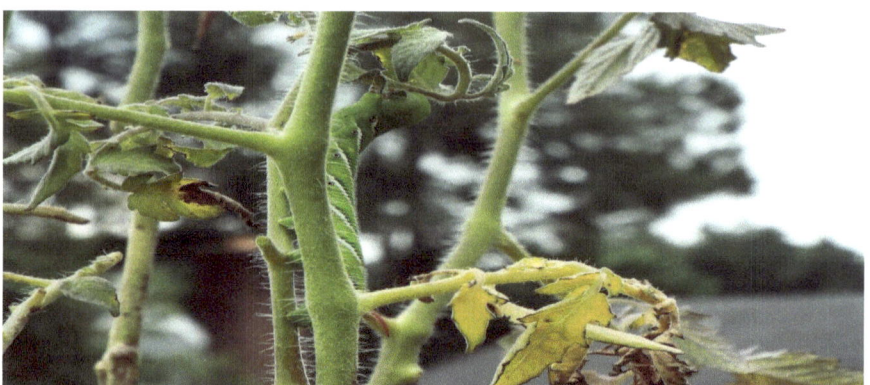

North Carolina- Carolina del Norte

Tobacco Hornworms are well camouflaged among the leaves of my tomato plant. Look closely at the white diagonal lines to "see" the Tobacco Hornworm. This is the late instar larva stage. The Tobacco Hornworms eats nectar and becomes a moth. The writer chose the photo opportunity rather than pluck the Tobacco Hornworm off the tomato vine. (entnemdept.ufl. /edu/creatures/field/tobacco_hookworm)

Los anquilostomas de tabaco estan bien camuflados entre las hojas de mi planta de tomate. Mire de cerca las lineas diagonals blancas para ver el anquilostomas de tabaco. Esta es la etapa tardia de la larva del instar. El anquilostoma de tabaco come nectar y se convierte un polilla. Es escritor eligios la oportunidad de tomar fotos en lugar de arrancar el Gusano del tobacco de la vid de tomate

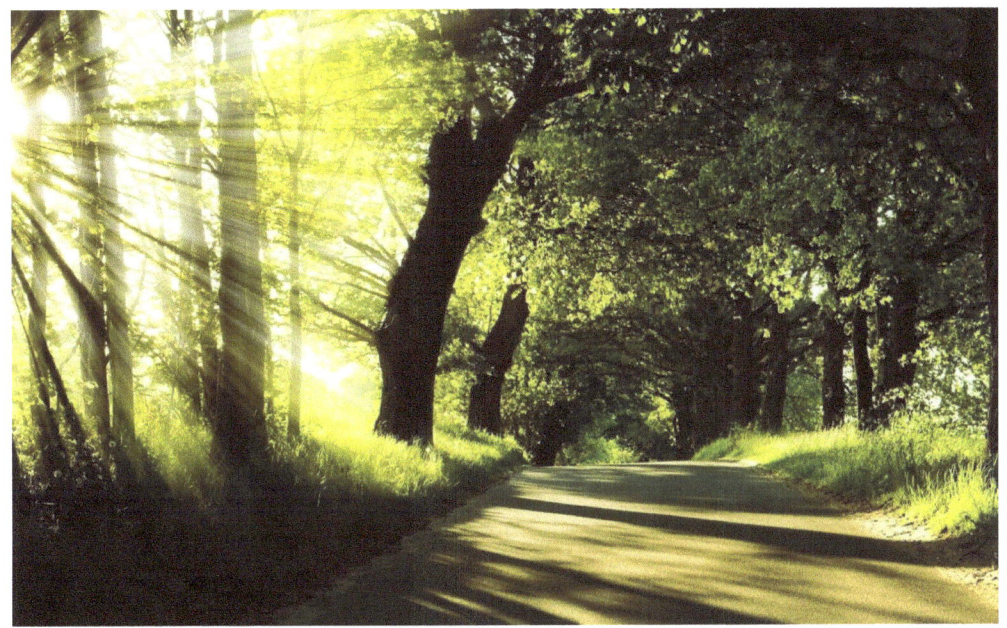

This Photo by Unknown Author is licensed under CC BY-SA-NC

Not how long, but how well you have lived is the main thing.

No cuanto tiempo, sino que tan bien has vivide es el pensamiento principal

                                        Seneca

Be Happy for this moment. This moment is your life.

Ser feliz por este momento. Este momento es tu vida

                                        Omar Khayyam

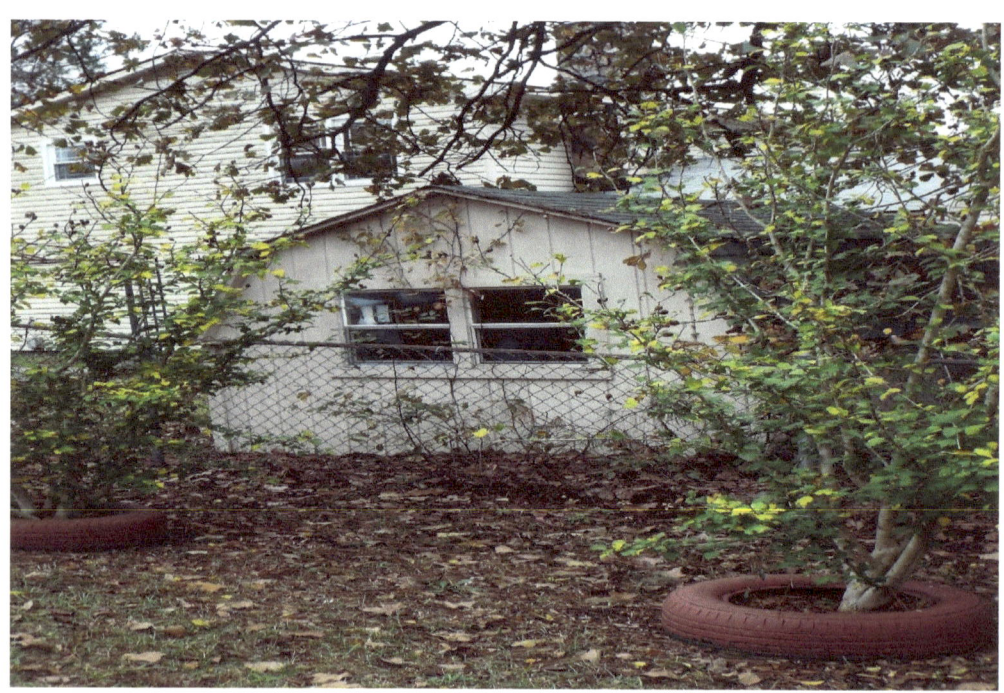

North Carolina – Carolina del Norte

Home of garden and lawn equipment

Hogar para herramientas de jardineria y equipos de jardineria

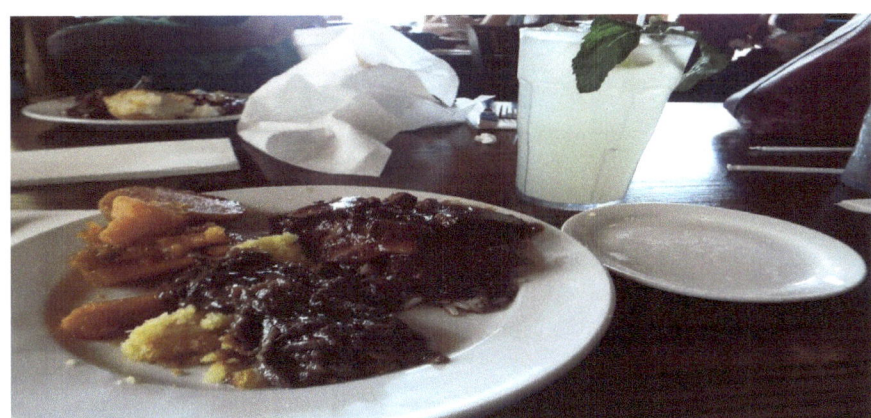

Lady and Sons -Damas e hijos Savannah, Georgia

The South is where mint lemonade is sweet, and accents are sweeter; summer starts in April; front porches are wide, and words are long. Pecan pie is a staple. Someone is always getting their heart blessed.

El sur es dondes la limonada de menta el dulce y los ascentos son mas dulce; el Verano comienza en abril; los porches son anchos y las palabras son largas, el pastel de nueces es un alimento basico, Alguien siempre esta bendiciendo su corazion

(the southernladycooks.com)

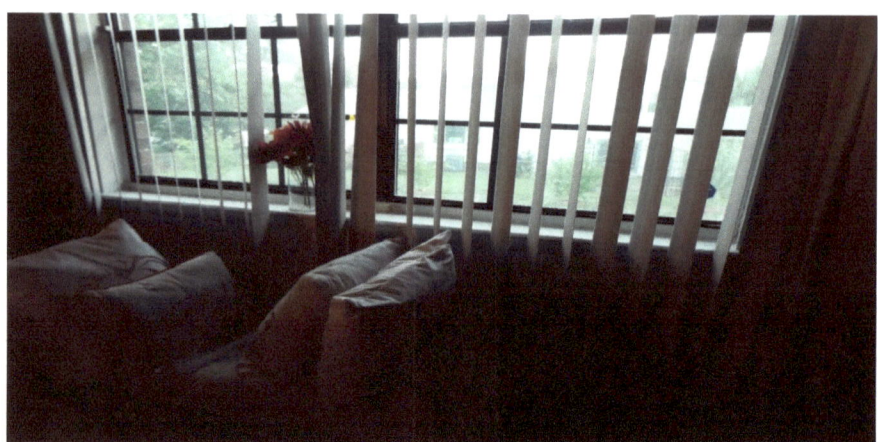

North Carolina -Carolina del Norte

A window seat is the me time area. One can read, look at the trees and plants in the yard. Sometimes wasps, mosquitos, and dragonflies splat against the window. Blonde Squirrels run across the yard to the long leaf magnolia trees. The writer often listens to the rain during inclement weather and birds on the sunlit days. Quiet beautiful area has fluffy throw pillows for hugging and reclining for cloud-watching. Dreams, visioning, and centering on peace after a chaotic day on the window seat. Affirmations on Throw pillows surround me in the words of gratitude such as Thankful. Me time reflection is such a gift to myself.

Un asiento junto a la ventena es el area de tiempo de mi. Uno puede leer, mirar arboles y plantas en el patio. Ardillas rubias corren por la patio hacia los abroles de magnolia de hojas larga. El escritor a menuedo escucha al lluvia durante el mal tiempo y las aves en los dias soleados. Una zona tranquila y hermosa tiene almohadas mullidas para abrazarse y recostarse y observer la nubes. Suenos, visionar, y centrarse en la paz despues de un dia caotico en el asiento de la Ventana.

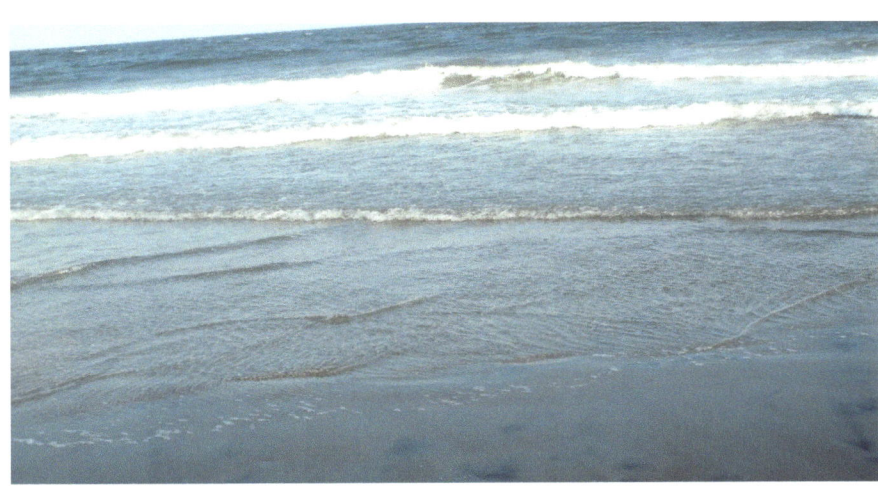

Tybee Island, City in Georgia- Atlantic Ocean View. Tybee Island is a barrier island and small city. Fort Screven has 19th century concrete gun batteries and Tybee Island Light Station and Museum. The still functioning 18th century lighthouse has been rebuilt many times and the Battery Garland. The city-island features marine science centers. Walk on the beach, learn about sea turtles or trek through the marsh (https://www.tybeemarinescienceorg)(en.m.wikipedia.org/wiki/ Tybee Island Georgia History

Tybee Island, ciudad en Georgia, vista al oceano Atlantico. Tybee Island es una isa barrera y pequena ciudad. Fort Screven tiene baterias de pistolas de hormigon del siglo XIX y la estacion de luz y museo Tybee Island. El faro que un funciona has sido reconstruido muchas veces el Battery Garland. La ciudad-isla cuenta con centros de ciencias marinas. Camina por la playa, apprendre sobre las tortugas marinas o camina por el pantano.

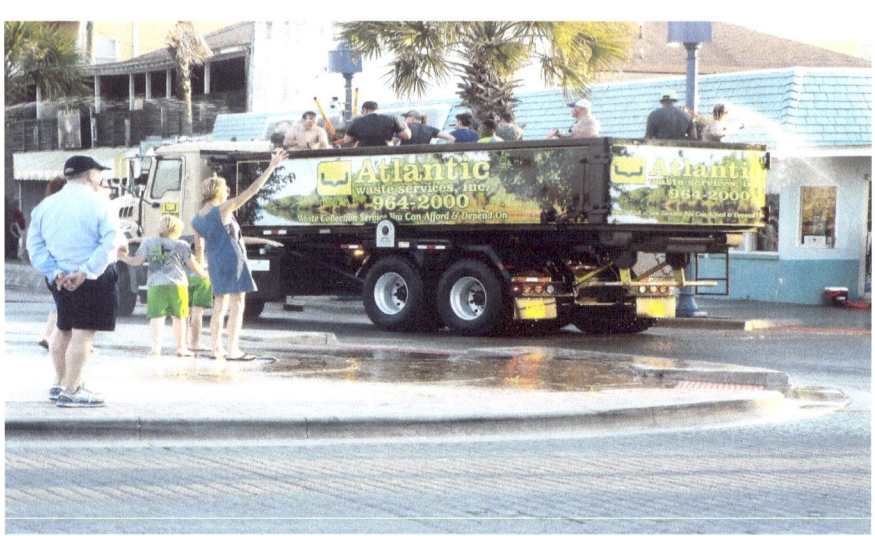

Tybee Island – Isla Tybee

Tybee Island Beach Bum Parade is a free event for locals and visitors. The parade goes down Butler Avenue and features island-wide water fights! The free event is usually 2 or 3 weeks before Memorial Day. Kids and adults with a sense of humor enjoy the water fights. The water fights have the intensity of paintball. The required gear are assault-size water guns, containers of iced water to refill the guns, bathing suits, ponchos, and eye protection. Everyone is fair game including the writer.(https://tybeeisland.com/events/event.beach-bum parade)

Tybee Island Beach Bum Parade es un evento gratuito para locales y visitants. Es desfile baja por la Avenida Butler y presenta luchas acuaticas todas la isla. Los combates acuaticos tienen intensidad del paintball. El equipo requerido una pistola de aqua de tamano de asalto, contenedores de aqua helda para rellenar las armas, trajes banos, ponchos y proteccion para los ojos. Todos el mundo es un juego justo, incluido el escritor.

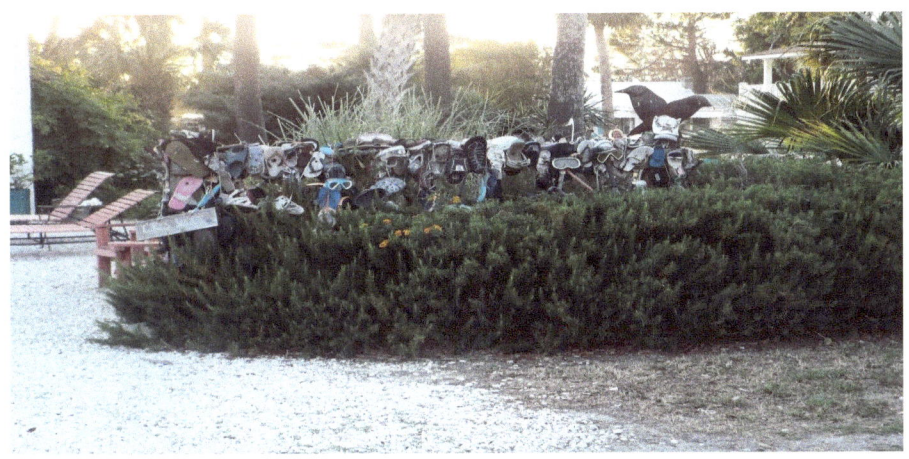

Tybee Island – Isla Tybee

Folk Art Sculpture of beach shoes and water gear represents the playful atmosphere of Tybee Island, Georgia

La escultura de arte popular de zapatos de playas ropas aqua representa la atomsofera ludica de Tybee Island, Georgia

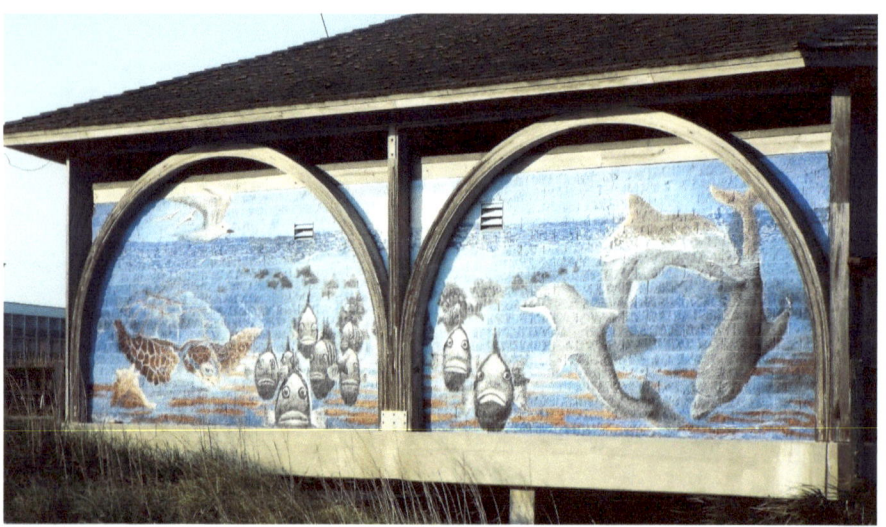

Dolphin mural from Tybee Island, Georgia – Mural del delfines de Tybee Island, Georgia

The happiness of the bee and the dolphin is to exist. For man {people} it is to know that and wonder at it.   Jacque Yves Cousteau

La Felicidad de la abeja y el delfin es existir. Para la gente es saber eso y mararvillarse.

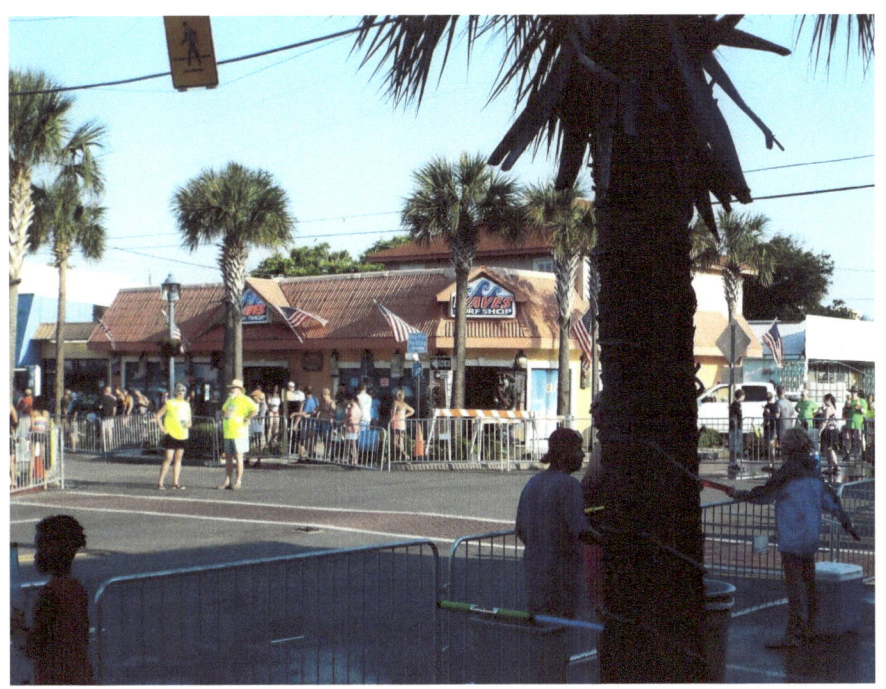

Tybee Island – Isla Tybee

Waiting for the Tybee Island Beach Bum Parade and water fight war preparations. Ready! Aim! Fire!

Esperando el Tybee Island Beach Bum Parade y la preparacion de la querra luchar contra el aqua. Listo! Objetivo! Fuego!

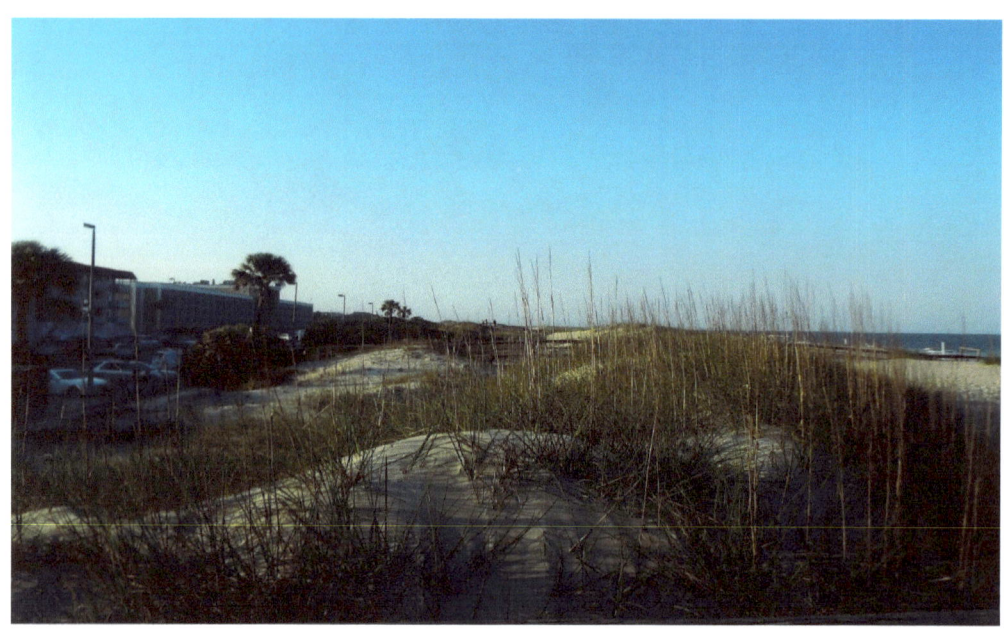

Sand dune borders of mouth of the Savannah River of Tybee Island, Georgia.

Dunas de arena bordean la desembocadura del rio Savannah

In this big ball of people, I am just one grain of sand in this beach

Aurora

En esta un gran bola de gente, solo soy un grano de arena en una playa.

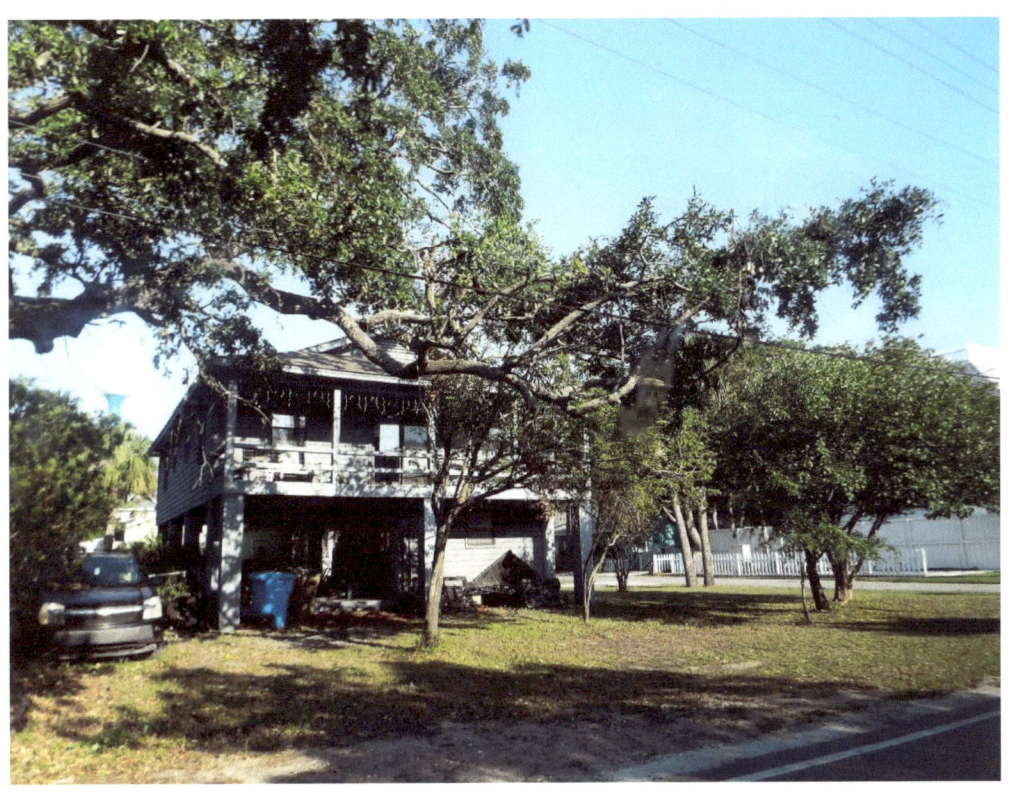

Home on Tybee Island. Georgia – casa en Tybee Island, Georgia

Light, God's eldest daughter, is the principal beauty in a building.

Thomas Fuller

La Luz, hija mayor de Dios, es en la belleza principal de un edificio.

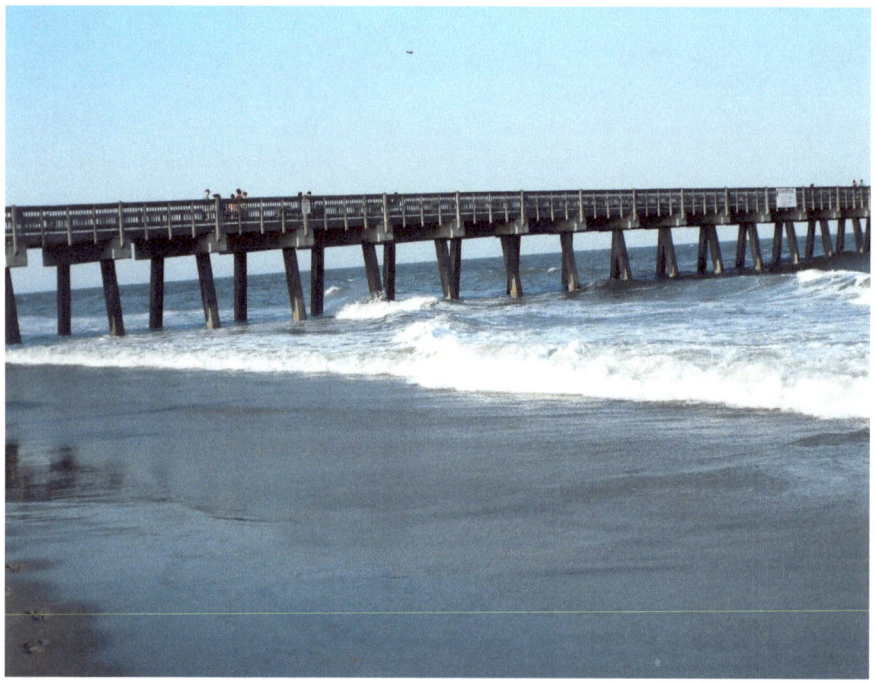

Tybee Island, Georgia boardwalk across the mouth of the Savannah River

Isa de Tybee, paseo maritimo de Georgia a traves de la desembocadura del rio savannah

Standing on the boardwalk and feeling the spray of the waves on your face. Hearing the wave song with each movement of the water. Seeing the white crests merge and expand upon breaking on sand. Feeling the sand between your toes from the walk from the beach to the boardwalk. Recalling the history of the profitable rice export in coastal Georgia and slaves who died from disease were buried on the west end of Tybee Island (Atlantic Slave Trade to Savannah, georgiaencyclopedia.org)

De pie en la acera y sintiendo el Rocio de las olas en tu cara. La sensacion de arena entre los dedos de los pies. Recordando la historia del arroz y los esclavos. Los esclavos que murieron por enfermedad fueron enterrados en el extremo oeste de las isla Tybee

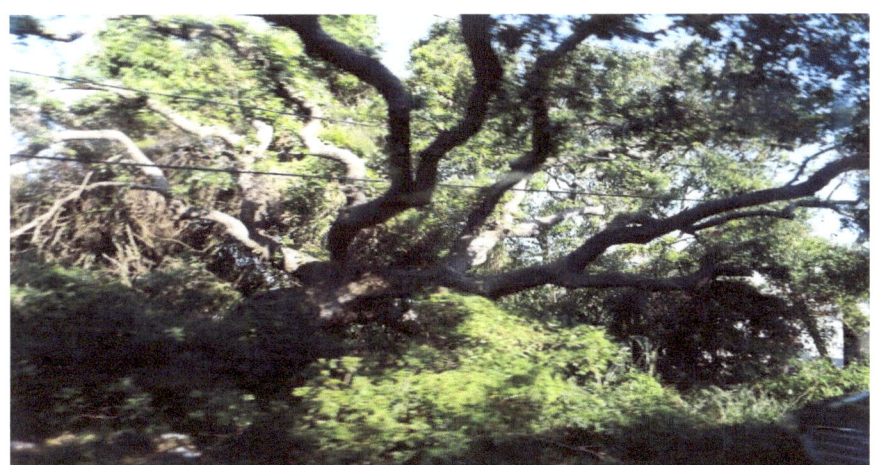

Barrier islands in the Charleston are a different geographical structure than Sea Islands The barrier islands in the Charleston area have nothing between the ocean and the island. It is a longer boat ride to the ocean but often sit at a higher elevation and are more protected from a tidal surge. When the sea level rises, barrier islands develop in the mouth of bays along certain types of coast lines. (Barrier Island vs. Sea Island -Debby

La islas de barrera en Charleston tienen una estructura geografica diferente a las islas del Mar. Las islas de barrera no tiened nada entre el oceano las isla. Cuando el nivel del mar sube, las islas de barrera se deasrrollan en las bocas de las bahias.

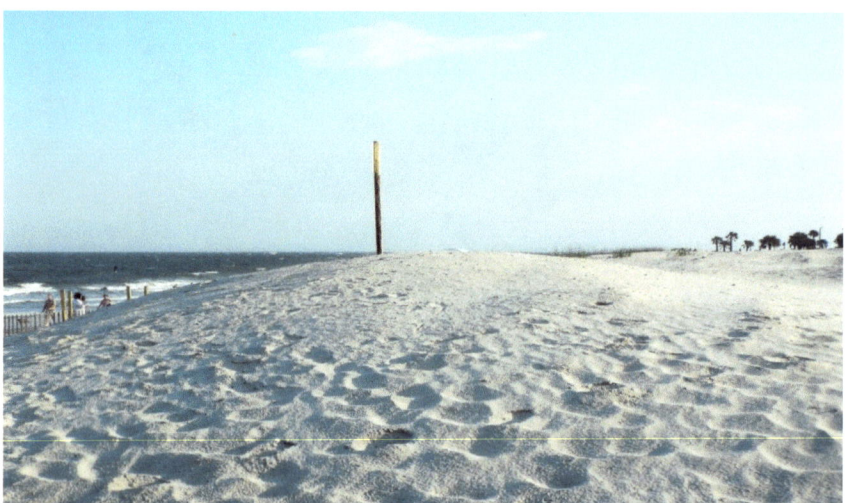

Sea Islands are formed when the tops of the volcanoes appear above the water. The volcano is still beneath the ocean surface, it is called a seamount. There are about 100 sandy islands off the Atlantic coast of southeastern United States. (Britannical.com>place>Sea-Islands.)

La islas del mar se forman cuando las cimas de los volcanes aparecen sobre el aqua. El volcan todavia esta debajo de la superficie del oceano, se llama monte submarino. Hay approximadamente 100 islas arenosas frente a la costa altlantica del sureste de los Estados Unidos.

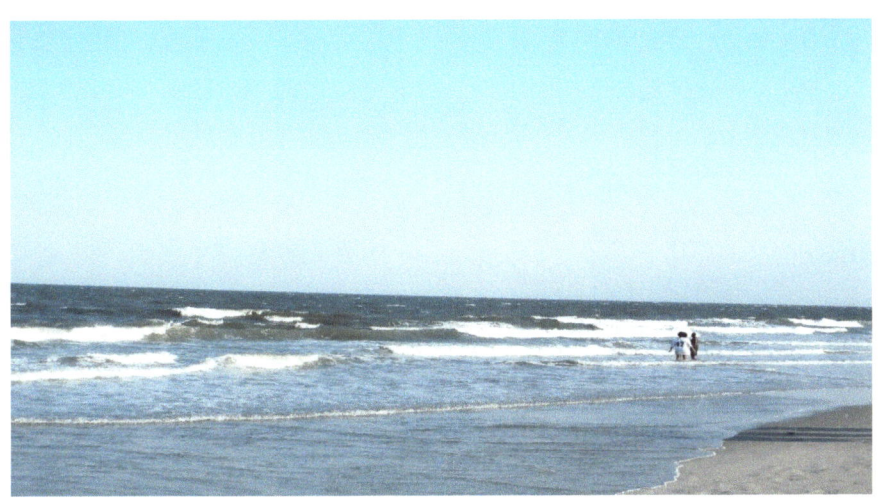

Geechee and Gullah is the unique culture of enslavled Central and West Africans. Geechee and Gullah people have inhabited the Sea Islands for centuries. The Sea Islands are off the coasts North Carolina, South Carolina, Georgia, and Floridia.This area is known as part of the Gullah Geechee Corridor. Aspects of the culture thrives throughout the corridor and southern culture, which includes Hilton Head Island. The people are the descendants of rice plantation slaves.

Geechee y Gullah es las cultura unica de los esclavos de Africa Central y Occidental. Geechee y Gullah han habitado las islas de Mar durante siglos. Las islas del Mar estan frente a los costas de Carolina del Norte, del Carolina del Sur, Georgia, y Floridia. Esta area es parte del Corridor Gullah Geechee. Los aspectos de la cultura prosperan en todo el corredor y la cultura de sur, que incluye la Isla Hilton, Carolina del Sur. Las personas gullah y geechee son descendientes de esclavos de plantaciones de arroz

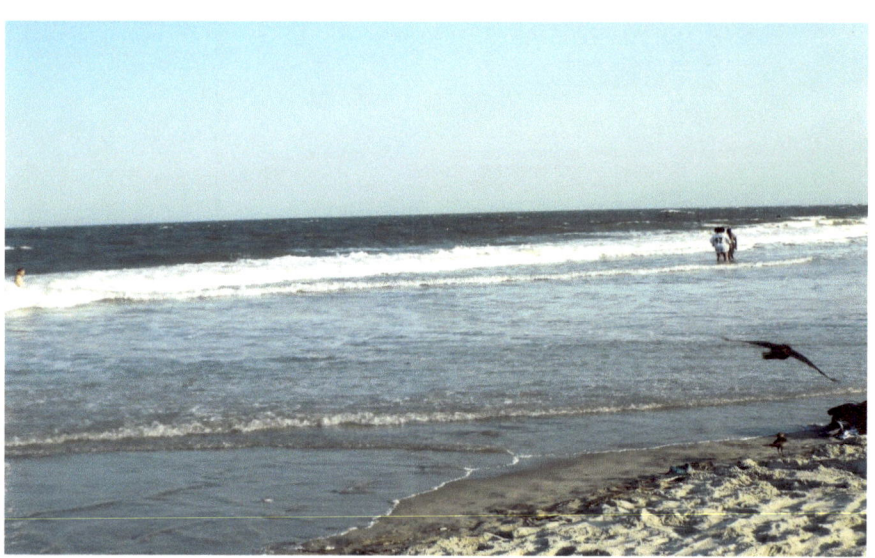

Daufuskie Island is a barrier island off the coast of South Carolina. It remains largely untouched by modern development. There are no grocery stores, no strip malls, no gas stations, and no bridge. One reaches the island by ferry by Hilton Head Ferry. Golf carts are the main mode of transportation. The beaches are gorgeous, beautiful art, and rich indigenous Gullah culture. (https: discoversouthcarolina.com/articles/Daufuskie-island.)

Daufuskie means "Land with a Point. "Daufa" means feather and "Fuskie "means pointed. (Dafuskie Island -Google)

Daufuskie Island es una isla arrecife de barrera de Carolina del Sur. Daufau significa pluma y fuskie significa puntiagudo. No hay centros centrales, estaciones de servicio, or puentes. Un viaja a la isla en ferry Hilton Head Island. Los carrittos de golf son el principal medio de transporte terreste. Las playas son hermosas, bellas artes y un rica cultura indigena de gullah

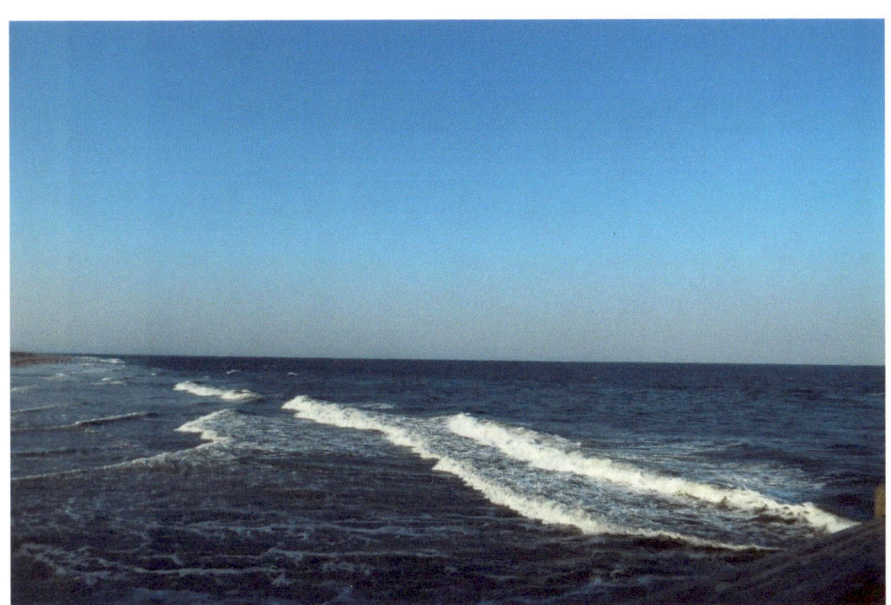

From Lake Hartwell the Savannah River flows southward over 300 miles, forming the Georgia/South Carolina border. It empties into the Atlantic Ocean near the city of Savannah. Along with the Tugaloo River, the Broad River is also a tributary of Savannah. The Savannah is an alluvial stream, meaning the waters originate in the mountains and Piedmont and flows across the Coastal Plains to the Ocean.(http://georgiaencyclopedi.org/articles/ Savannah-River)

Desede al lago Hartwell, el rio de Savannah fluye hacia el sur mas 300 millas, formando la frontera entre Georgia y Carolina del Sur. El rio Savannah es una corriente alluvial lo que significa que el aqua se origina en las montanas y Piedmount y fluye a traves de las llanuras costeras hacia el oceano.

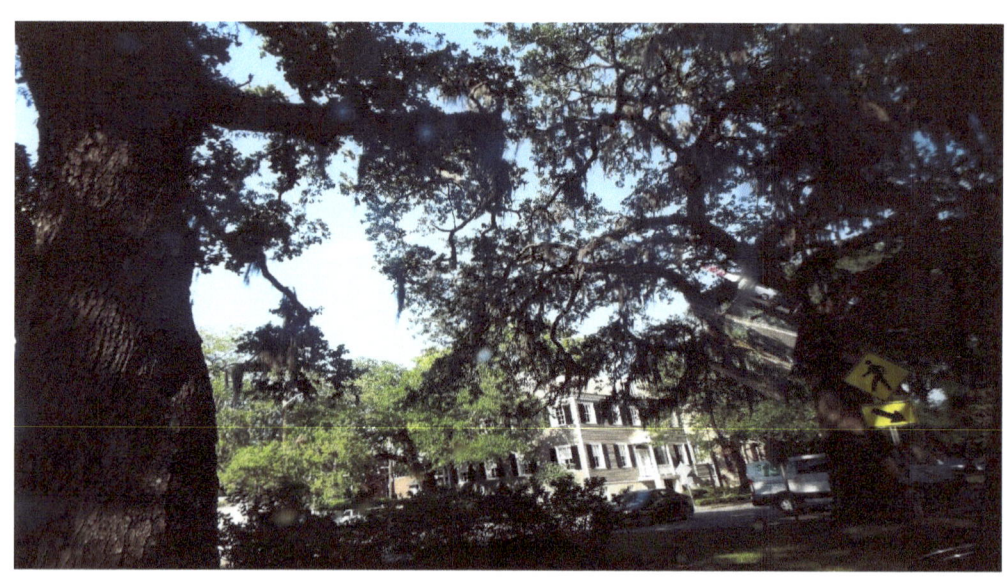

A view along the Savannah River

Una vista a lo del rio Savannah

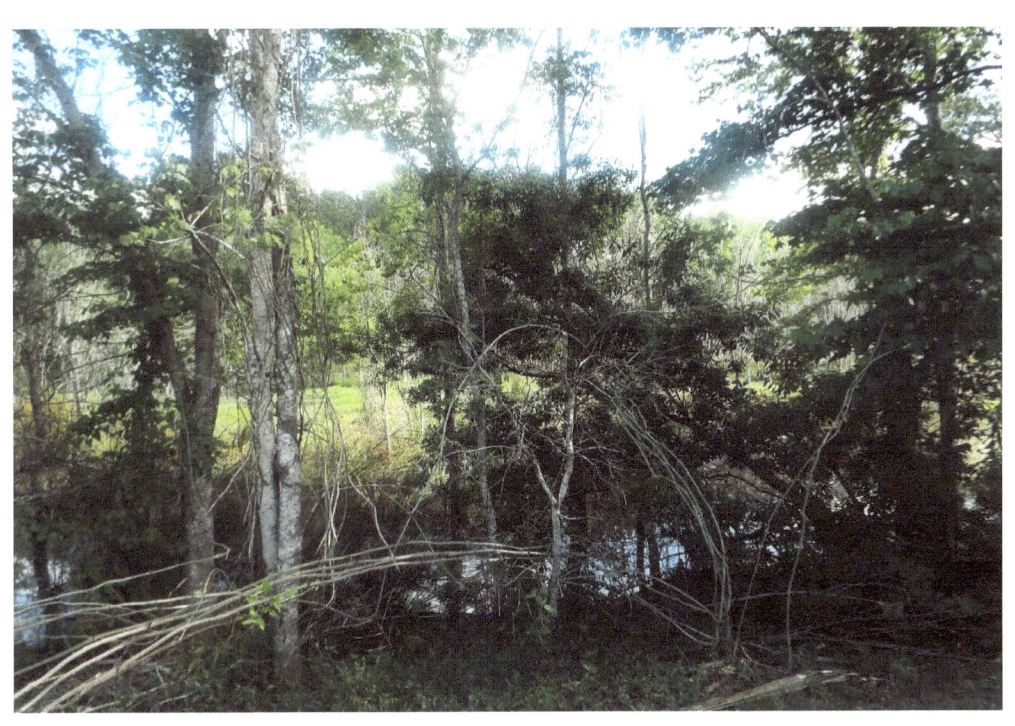

Woodland view of the Savannah River

Vista al bosque del rio de Savannah

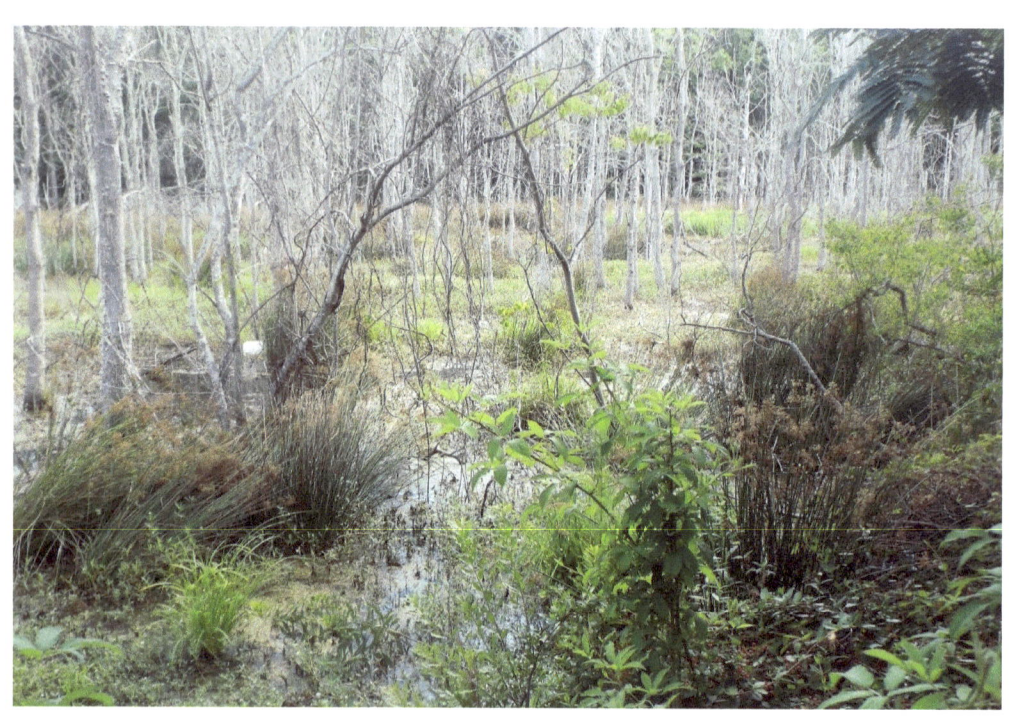

Marsh views of Savannah River, Georgia

Vistas del pantano del rio Savannah

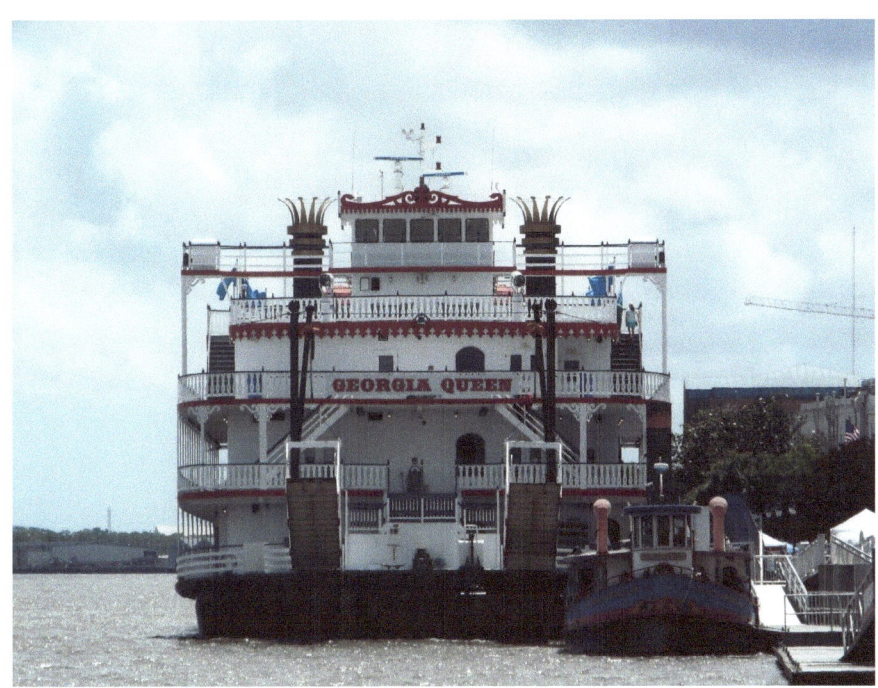

Savannah River Street -Calle del rio savannah

Savannah River Street has centuries old cotton warehouses converted to antique shops, boutiques, art galleries, pubs, nightspots, inns and hotels. The cruise on the Georgia Queen will provide sights of flowing Spanish moss hanging on oak trees. The Georgia Queen leaves dock next to the exact location where General Oglethorpe first landed on the Savannah river front(www.phillippublishing.com/issues/Savannah River

La calle Savannah River tiene alamacenes de algodon centenarios convertidos en tiendas de antiquedades, boutiques, galarias de arte, localales nocturnos, posadas y hotels. El crucero en el Georgia Queen proporcionara vista del musgo espanol que fluye en los robles. El Georgia Queen deja el muelle junto a la ubicacion exacta donde del general Ogelthorpe desembarci en el rio Savannah.

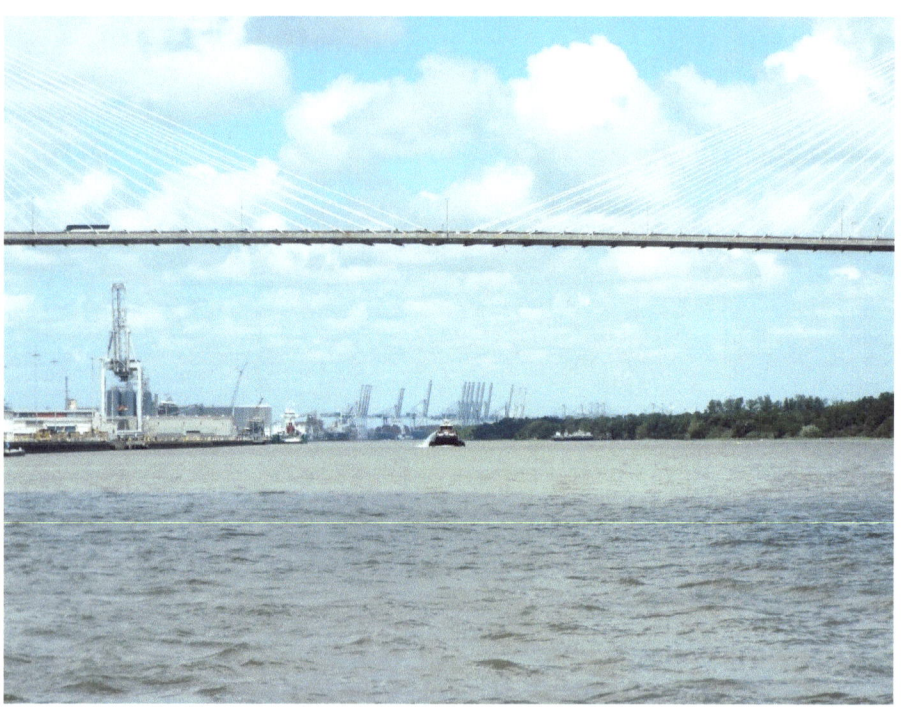

River Street, Savannah, Georgia -Calle del rio, Savannah, Georgia

Talmadge Memorial Bridge spans the Savannah River between downtown Savannah, Georgia, and Hutchinson Island. (Wikipedia >wiki>Talmadge Bridge

El Puente conmemorativo Talmadge atraviesa el rio Savannah entre centro de Savannah y la isla Hutchinson.

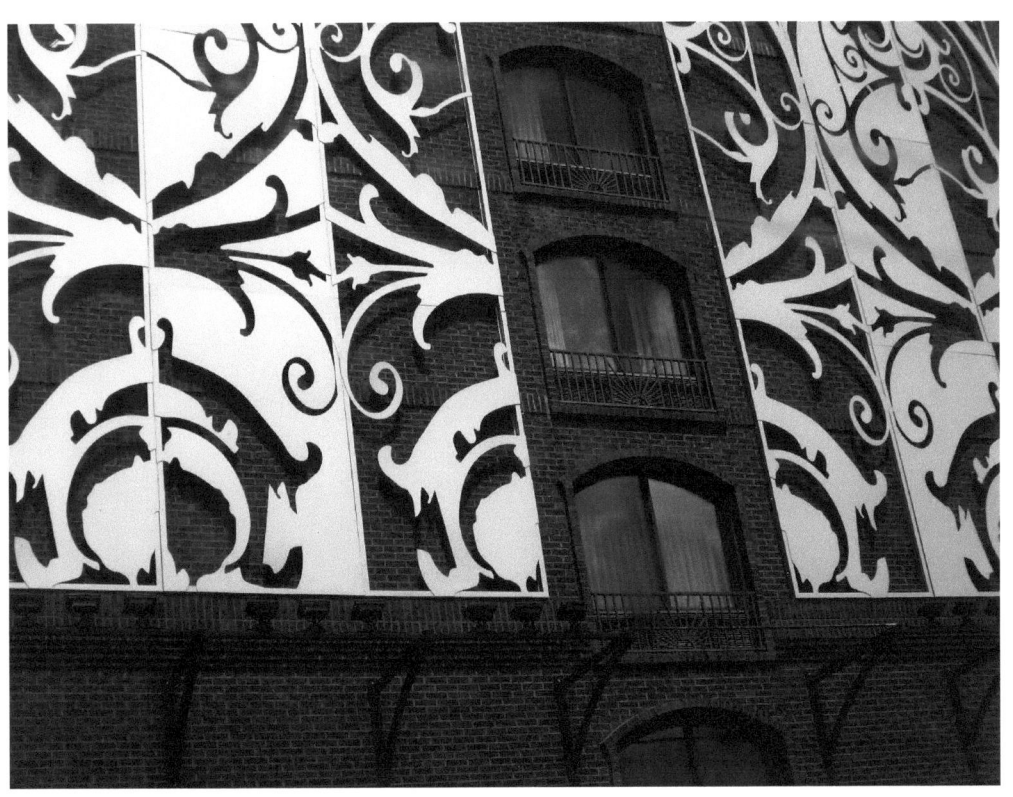

Savannah Historic District

Historical landmark

Hito historico de Savannah

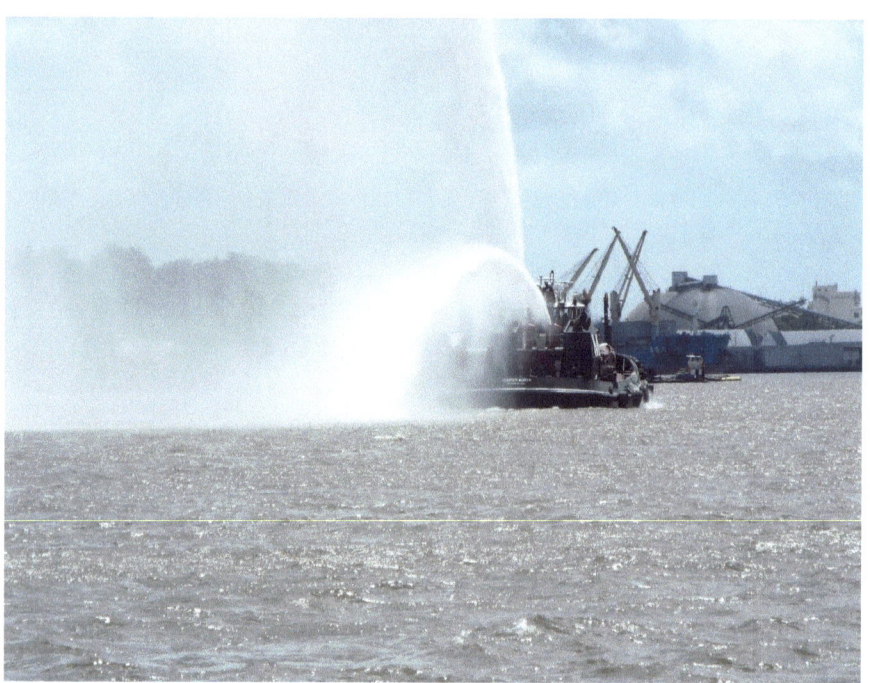

River Street Savannah, Georgia -Calle del rio Savannah

Savannah Georgia is a large, urban, historic district. The city limits and boundaries approximate pre-Civil War geography. (en.m.wikipedia.org/wiki/Savannah_History)

Savannah, Georgia es un gran distrito historico urbano. La geografia y limites se aproximan al periodo anterior a la Guerra civil.

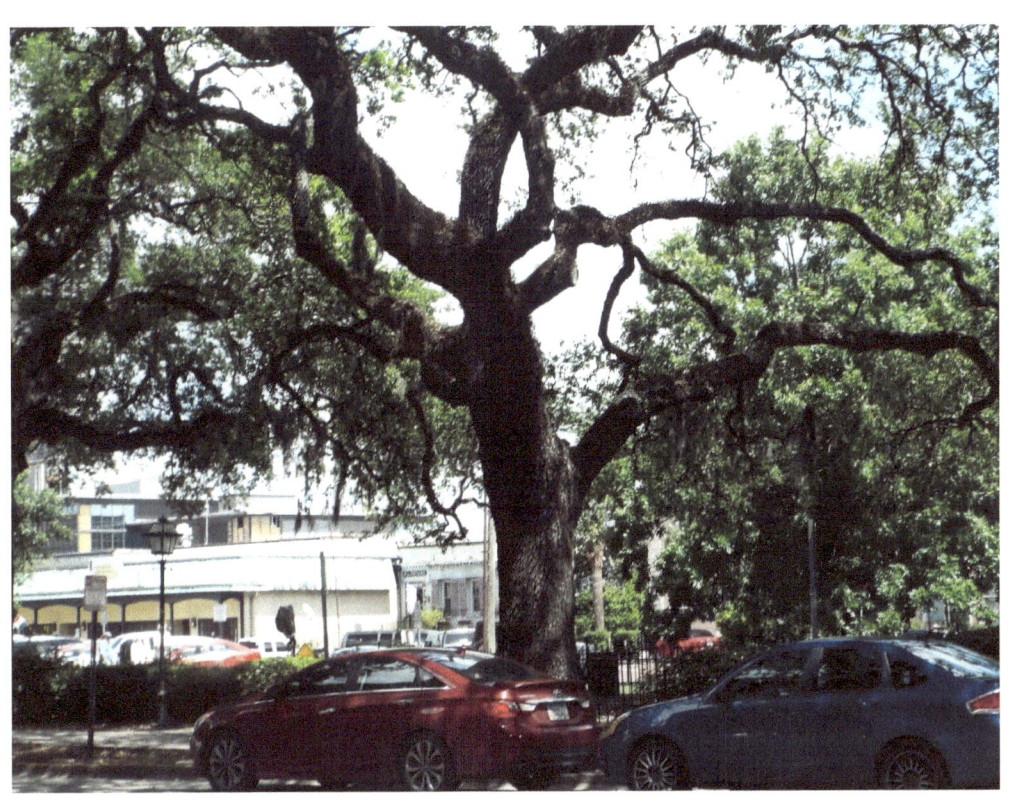

Savannah, Georgia Historic District-Distrito historico del Savannah, Georgia

The Savannah Historic District features 18th and 19th architecture and green spaces (en.m.wikipedia.org/wiki/Savannah_History.

El Distrito historico de Savannah, Georgia presenta arquitectura 18 y 19 y espacios verdes.

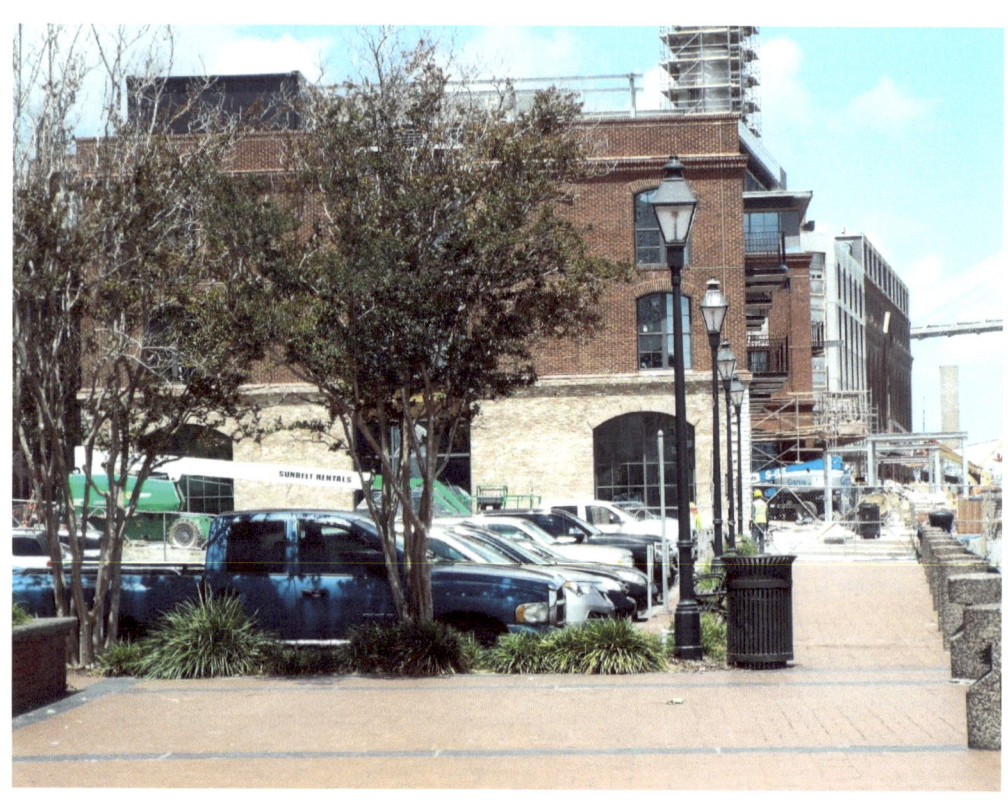

Savannah River Street-Calle del rio savannah

Cotton warehouses converted to tourist attractions such as restaurants and antique shops.

Almacenes del algodon convertidos en attraciones turisticas como restaurants y tiendas de antiquedades.

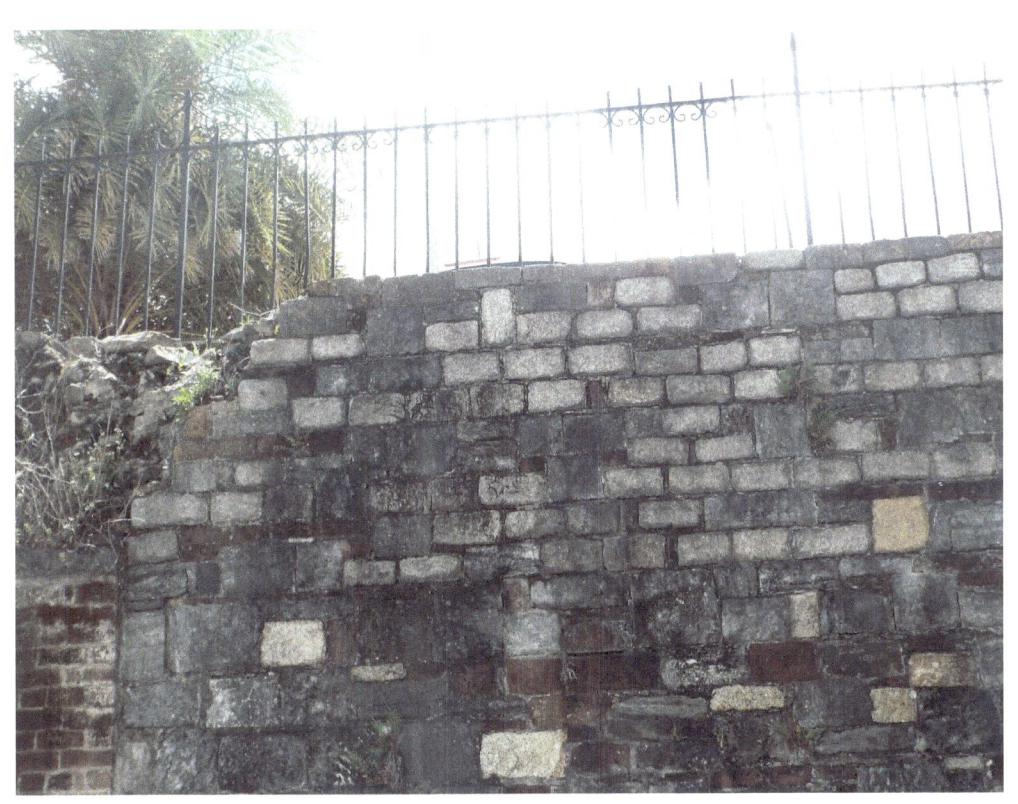

Savannah River Street Structure-Estructura de la calle rio Savannah

An 18th century wall on Savannah River Street

Un muro del siglo XVIII en la calle Savannah River

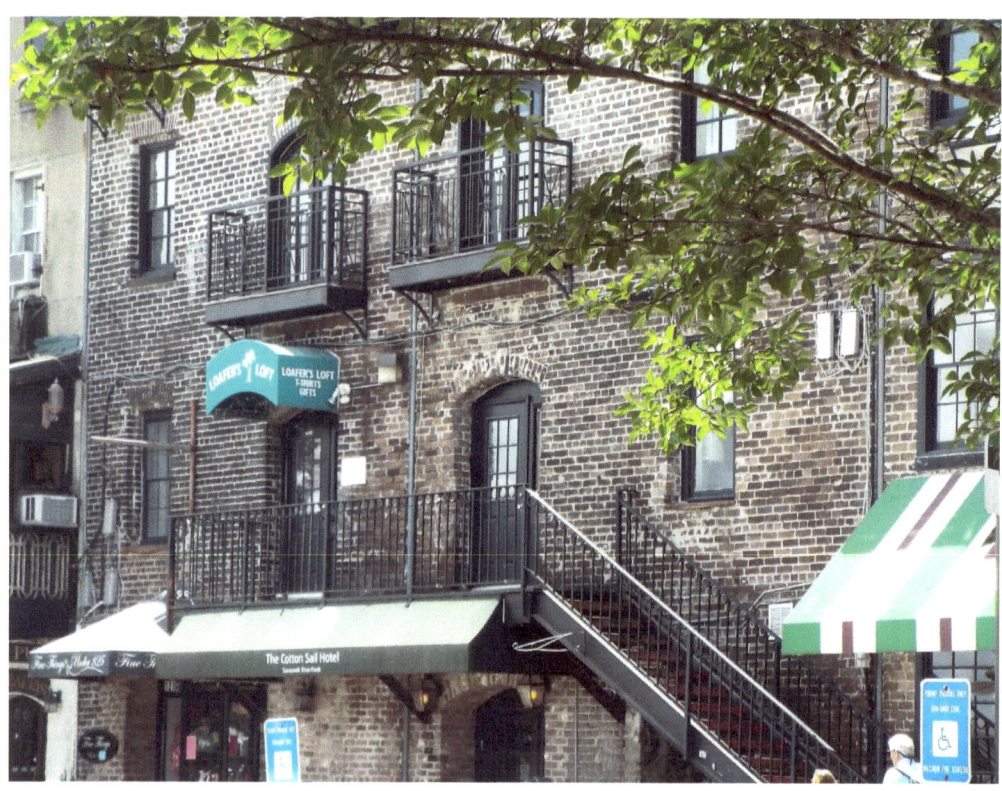

Savannah River Street Hotel-Hotel de la calle Savannah River

The Cotton Sail Hotel faces the Savannah River.

El hotel Cotton Sail da al rio Savannah.

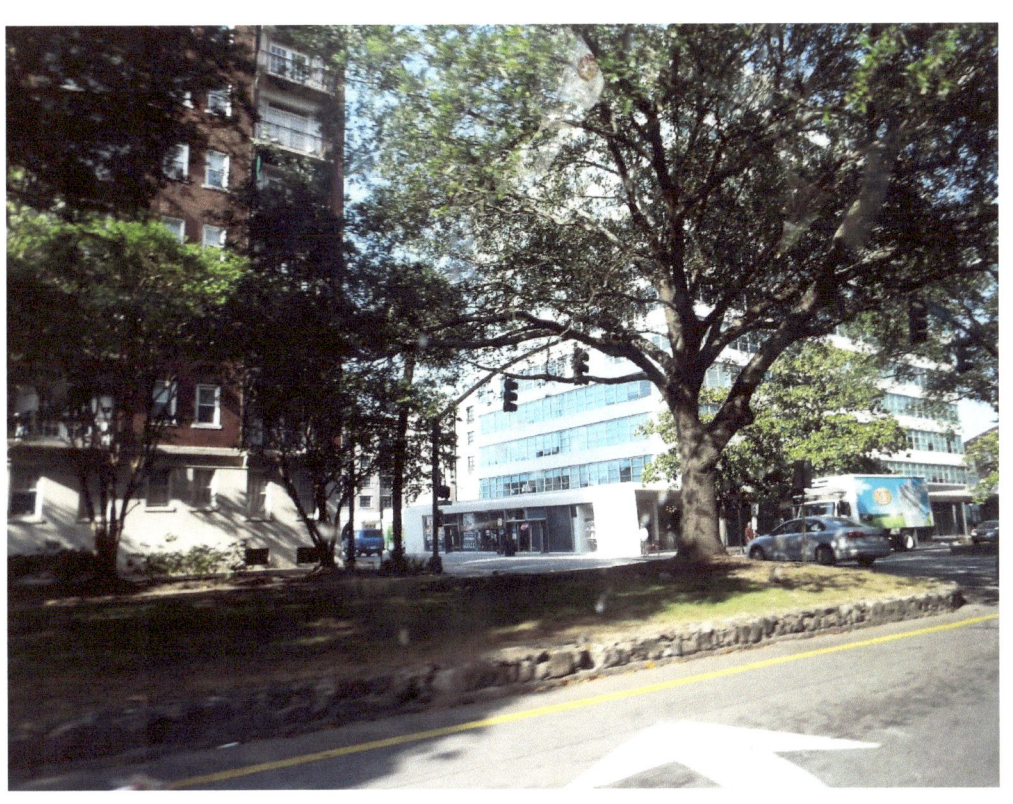

Downtown Savannah, Georgia-El centro de Savannah, Georgia

Green spaces are prevalent throughout the city.

Los espacios verdes prevalecen en toda la ciudad

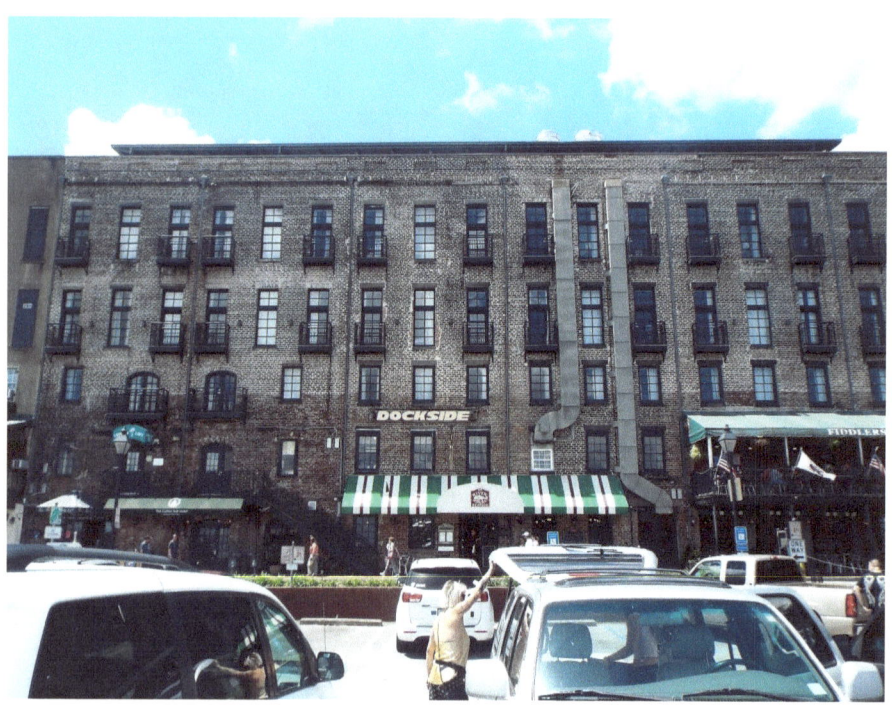

Savannah River Street -Dockside – calle del rio Savannah

The building was built in 1792 by Captain William Taylor, a ship chandler. It is the oldest existing ballast stone and masonry building in the state of Georgia, Along the Savannah waterfront are vestiges of old business sites, warehouses, and faded signs of taverns. Those were the days when Brown's Coffee House was fine and famous for enough for entertainment of George Washington. (https://www.docksideseafoodsav.com/AboutUs)

El edificio fur construido in 1792 por el capitan Willam Taylor, un vendedor be barcos. Es el edificio mas antiguo de ballas y mamposteria existente en el estado de Georgia. Esos fueron los dias en que Brown's Coffee House era suficientemente Bueno y Famoso para el entretenimiento de George Washington

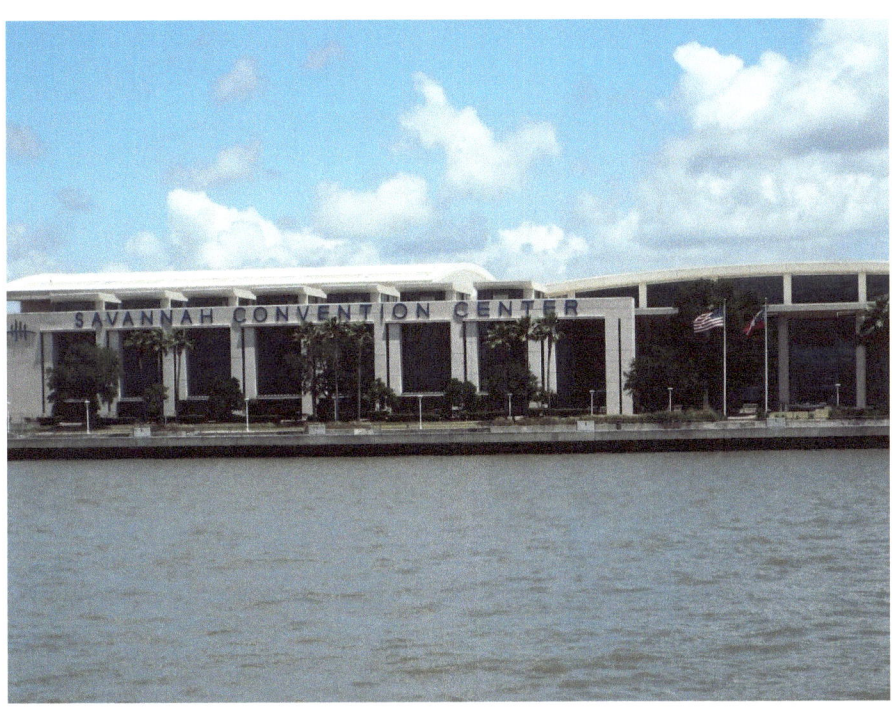

Savannah River Street-calle del rio Savannah

The Savannah Convention Center is located on Hutchinson Island. It has complimentary access by the Savannah Belles Water Ferry. (http://www.visitsavannah.com/profile/savannahconventioncenter)

El centro de convenciones de Savannah se encuentra en la isla Hutchinson. Tiene acceso gratuito por Savannah Belles Water Ferry.

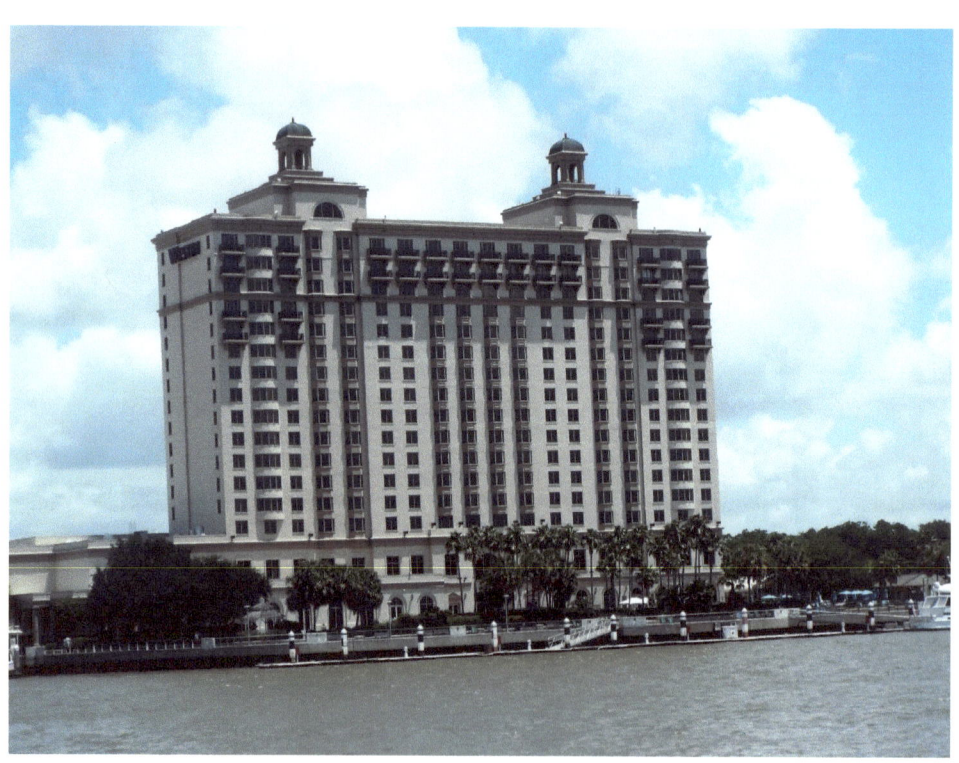

Savannah River Street

Calle del rio savannah

Westin Hotel on Hutchinson Island. Savannah Belles Ferry is a free way to see harbor and arrive at this hotel

Hotel Westin en la isla Hutchinson. El ferry de Savannah Belles es gratis para ver el puerto y llegar a este hotel.

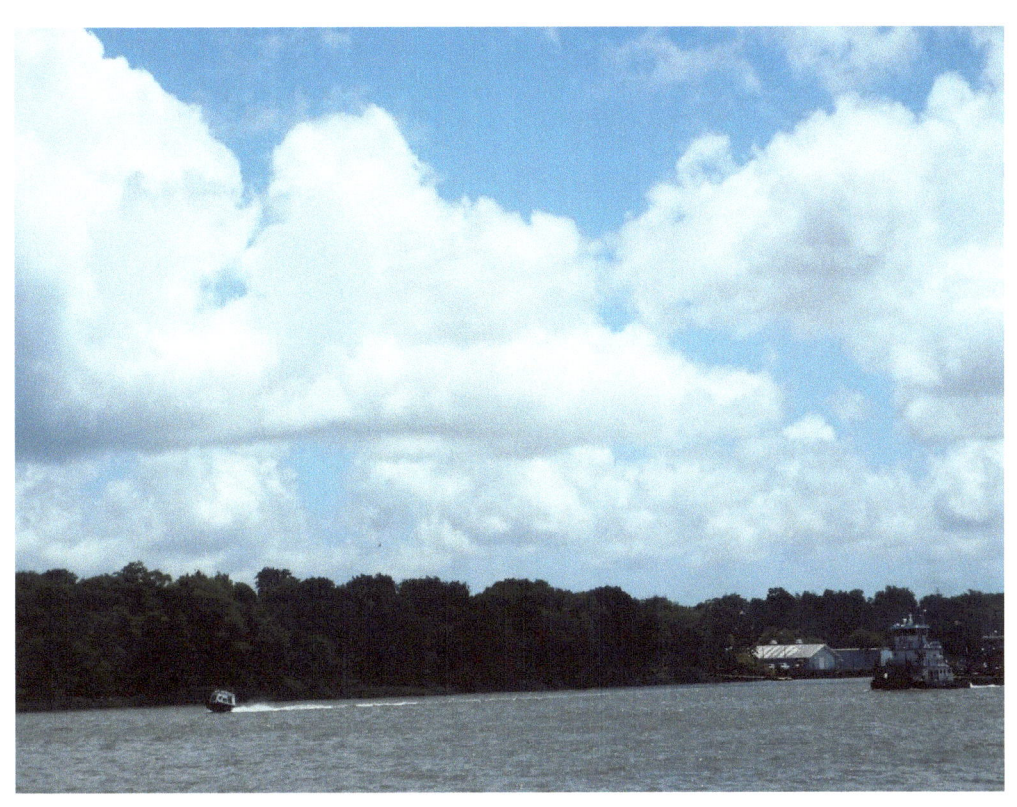

Savannah River

rio de Savannah

Coastal shore of Savannah River

Orilla costera del rio savannah

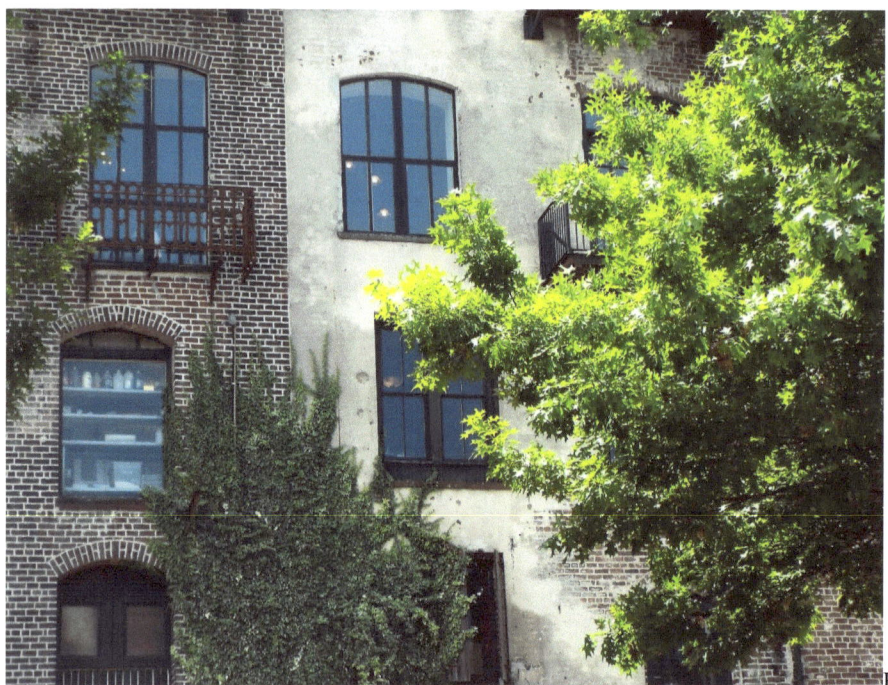

River Street, Savannah

Calle de rio Savannah

Windows facing Savannah River

Ventanas que dan al rio savannah

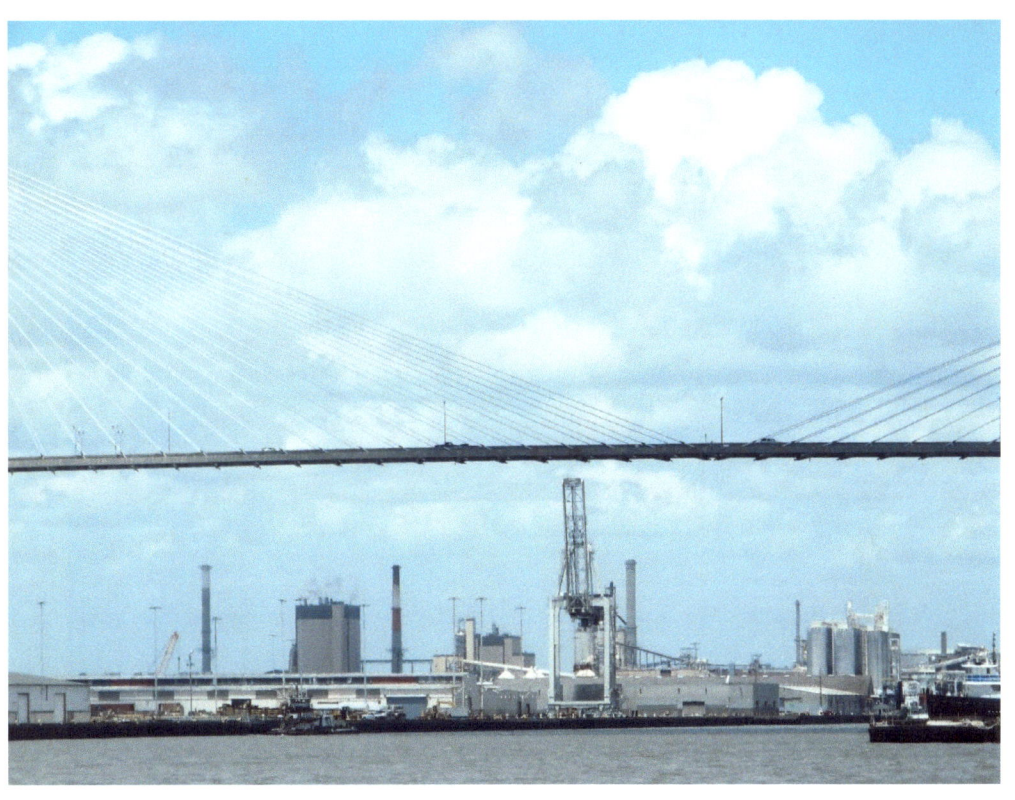

Calle de rio Savannah – River Street, Savannah Georgia

Talmadge Memorial Bridge across Savannah River

Talmadge Memorial Bridge a traves del Savannah

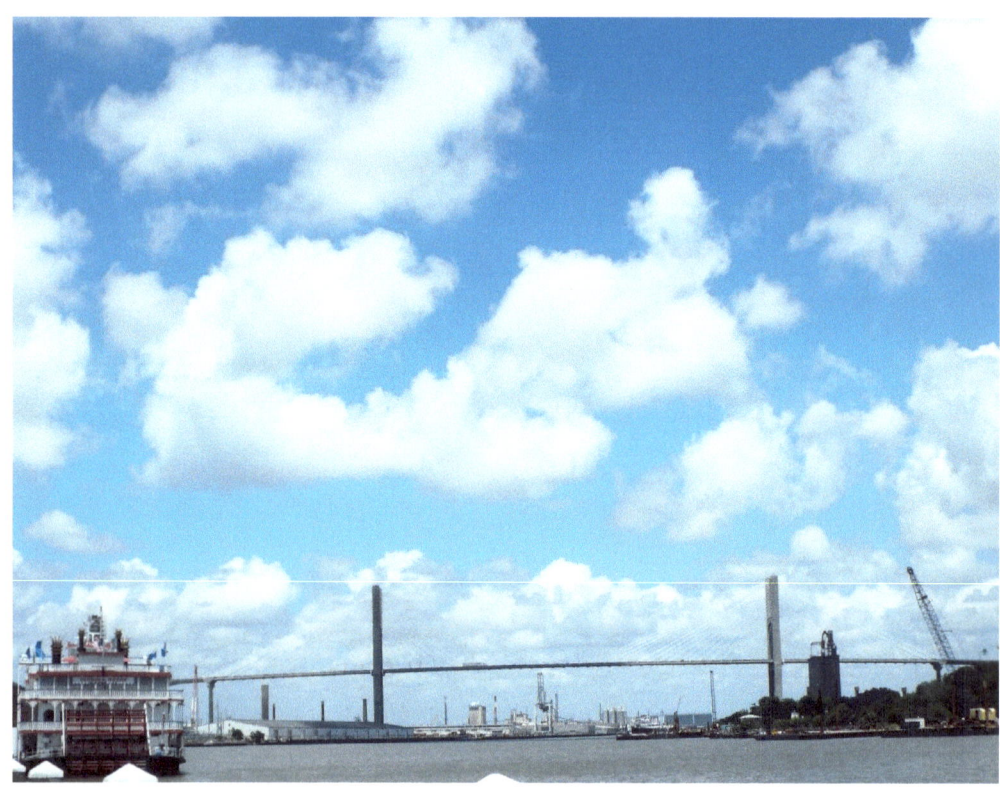

River Street, Savannah, Georgia

Calle del rio savannah, Georgia

Ferry and Talmadge Memorial Bridge

Ferry y Puente conmemorativo de Talmadge

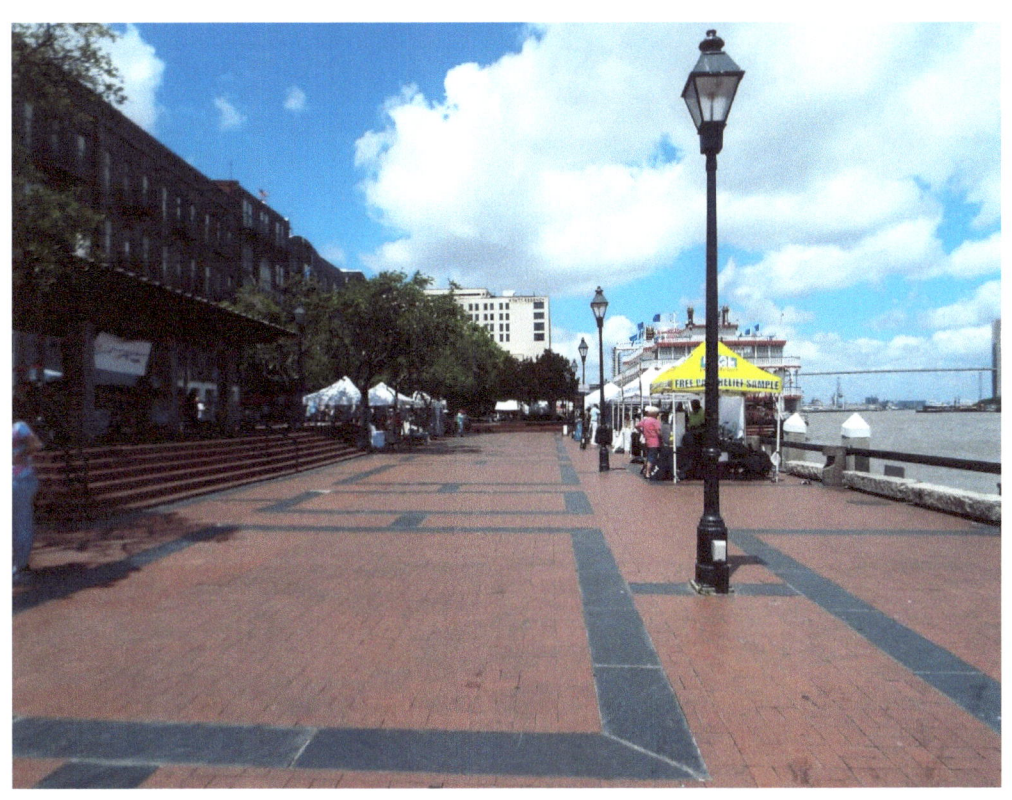

River Street, Savannah, Georgia

Calle del rio savannah, Georgia

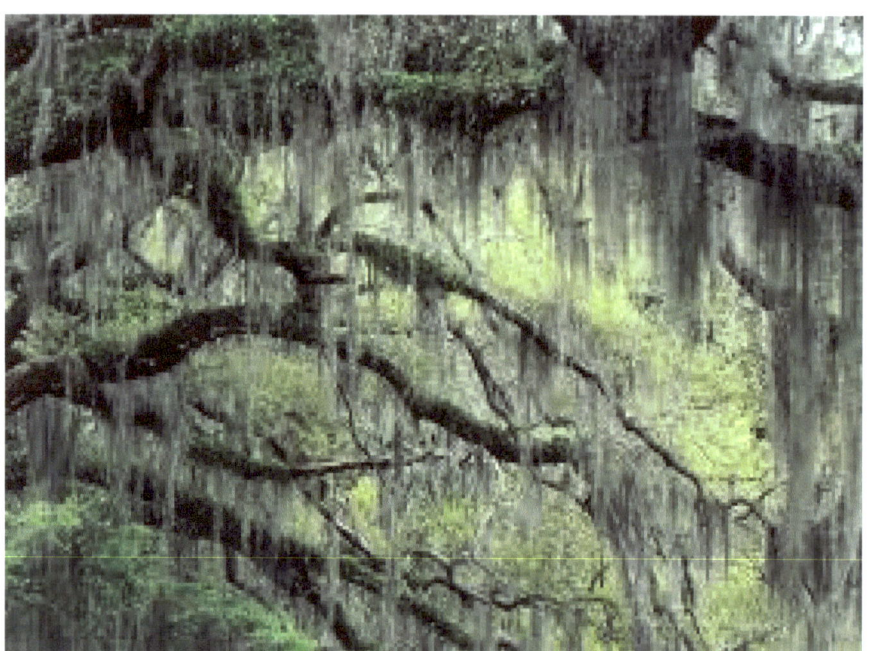

Savannah, Georgia Spanish Moss-Savannah, Georgia musgo espanol

Spanish moss is not a moss but a bromeliad-a perennial herb of the pineapple family. Spanish Moss are epiphytes. Epipthytes grow on other plants but do not rely on them for nutrients. They take nutrients from the air and the debris that collects on the plants. Spanish Moss grows in Mexico, Bermuda, Bahamas, Central America, South America, West Indies, and southern United states. (https:// en.m.wikipedia.org/wiki/Spanish_Moss)

Un musgo espanol no es un musgo, sino una hierba perenne bromelacea de la familia de la pina. El musgo espanol son epifitas. Las epifitas crecen en otras plantas pero no dependen ellas obtener nutrients. Toman nutrientes del aire y los desechos que se acumulan en la planta. El musgo espanol crece en Mexico, Bermudas, America Central, America del Sur, las Antillas, y el sur de los Estados Unidos.

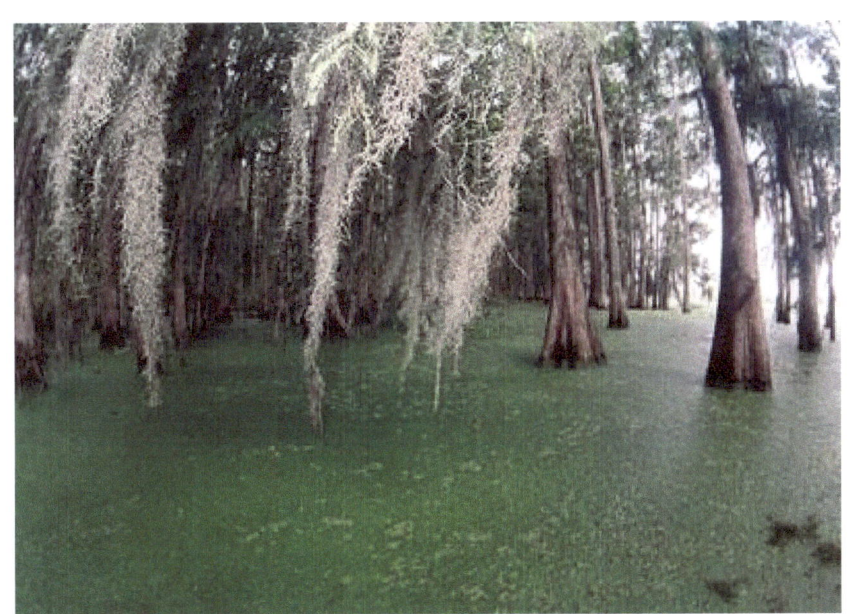

Florida Spanish Moss – Florida musgo espanol

The plant consists of one or more slender stems bearing alternate thin, curved, heavily scaled leaves in a pendant fashion. There are no aerial roots. The flowers are tiny, inconspicuous, brown green, and yellow (https://en.m.Wikipedia.org/wiki/Spanish Moss)

Las plantas consisten en uno o mas tallos delegado que tienen hojas alternas delgadas, curvadas y muy escamadas, de forma colgante. No hay raices aereas. Las flores son pequenas, discretas, marrones, verdes, y amarillas.

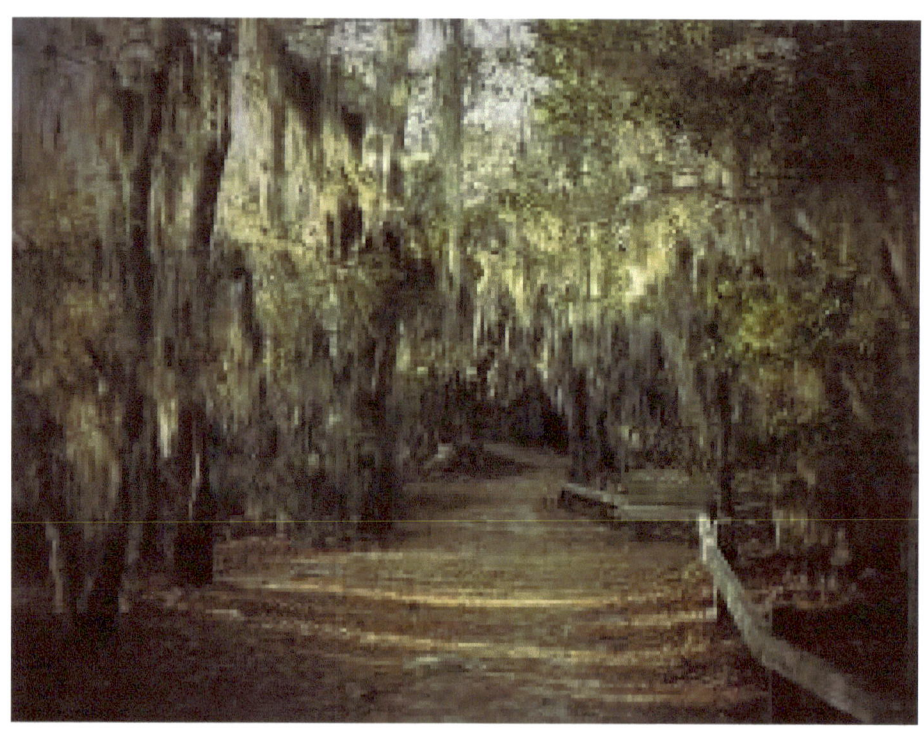

Virginia Beach Spanish Moss -Playa virginia musgo espanol (Viriginia)

Spanish Moss is not from Spain. It is a native plant of Mexico.

El musgo espanol no es Espana. Es una planta nativa de Mexico.

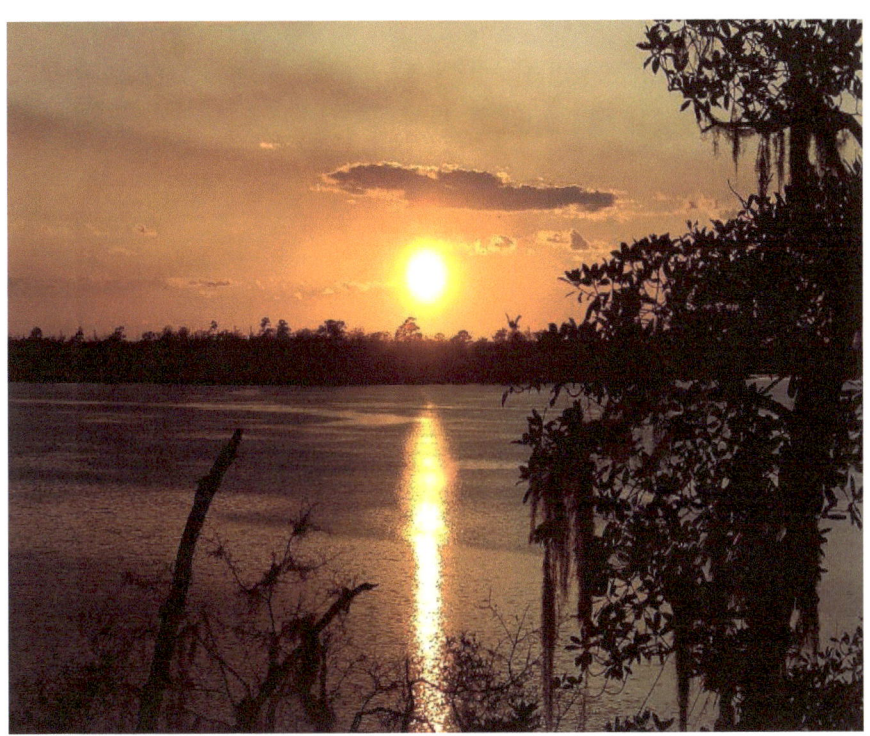

Alabama Spanish Moss-Alabama musgo espanol

Spanish Moss was given the name by French explorer. Native Americans told them the plant was called "Itla-okla" which meant "tree hair." The French were reminded of the Spanish conquistadors 'long beards so they called it Barbe Espagnol or "Spanish Beard (google facts: how did Spanish get its name.)

El musgo espanol fue dado por es explorador frances. Los nativos americanos les dijeron que la planta se llamaba "Itla-okla" que significa "pelo de arbol." Los franceses recordaban las largas barbas de los conquistadores espanoles, por lo que la llamaron Barba espanola.

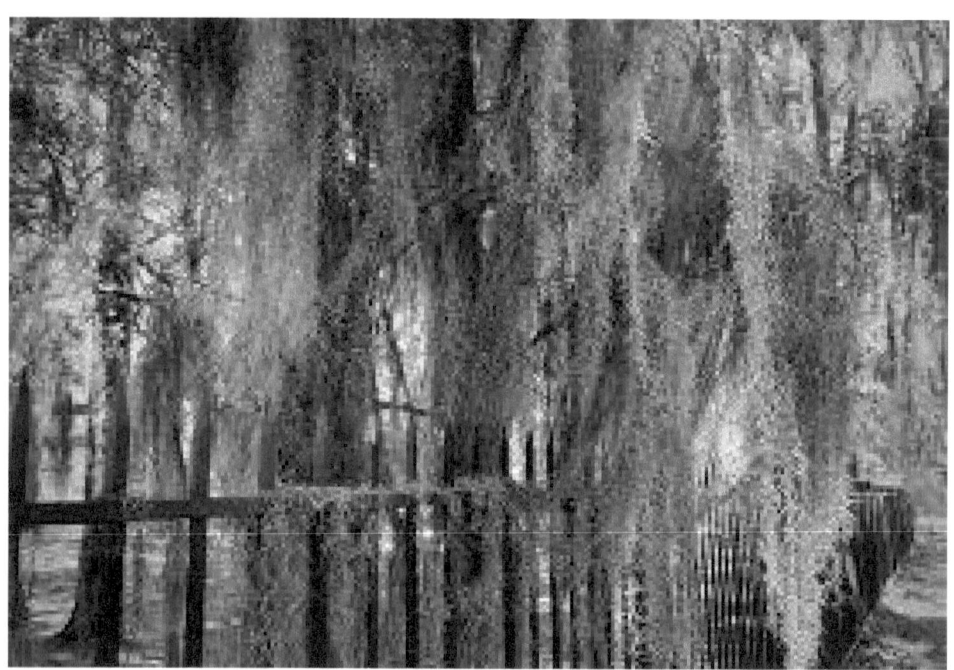

Mississippi Spanish Moss – Mississippi musgo espanol

Spanish moss plant has tiny scales that trap water until the plant can absorb it. Plant tissue can trap water until the plant can absorb it. When the tissues plumb up after the rain, Spanish moss appears greener. As water is used, it returns to a gray hue. (Mental Floss, 10 Things You Should Know About Spanish Moss, Miss Cellania, August 25, 2015)

El musgo tiene pequenas escamas que atrapan al aqua hasta que la planta puede absorberias. Cuando los tejidos se acumulan despues de la lluvia, el musgo espanol aparece mas verde. A medida que usa el aqua, Vuelve a un tono gris.

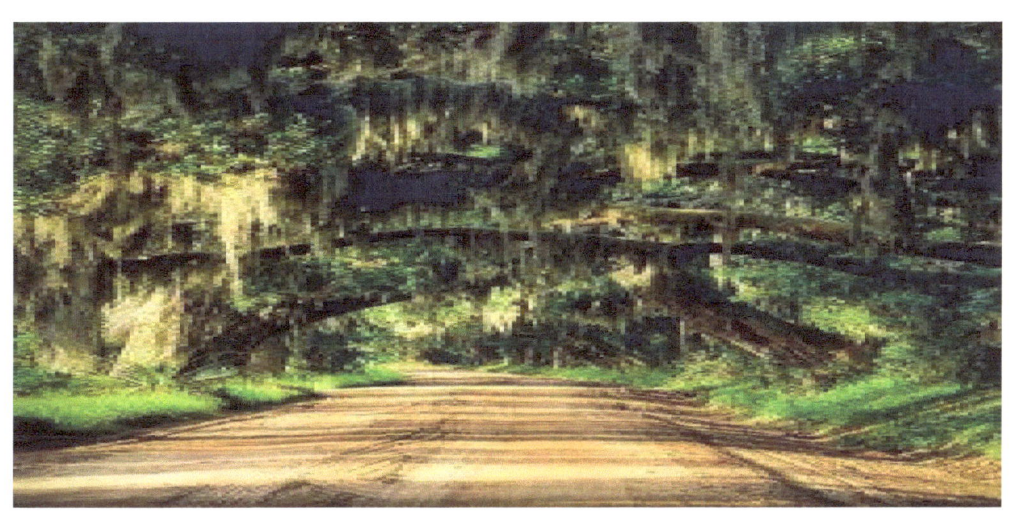

Edisto Island, South Carolina Spanish Moss -Isla Edisto, Carolina del Sur, musgo espanol

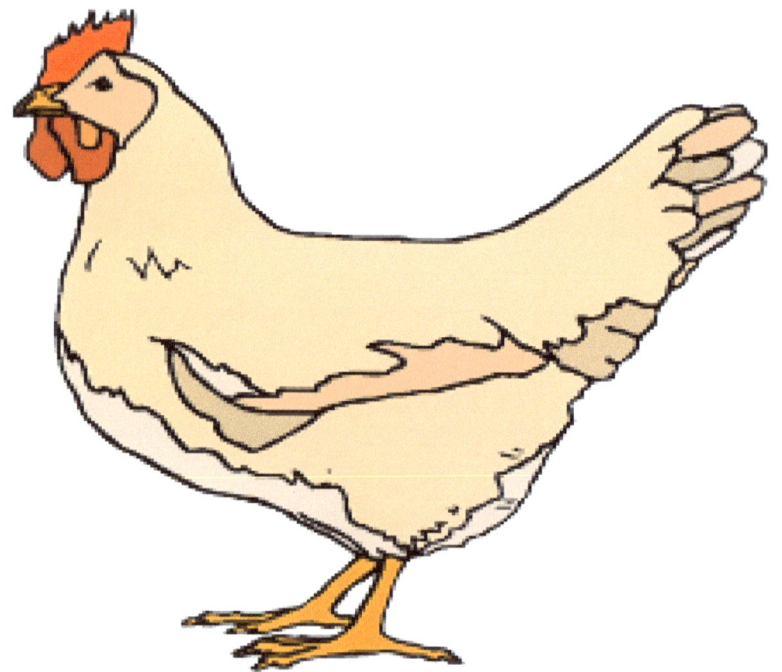

North Carolina -Carolina del Norte

Chickens are family pets – Los pollos son mascotas famillares.

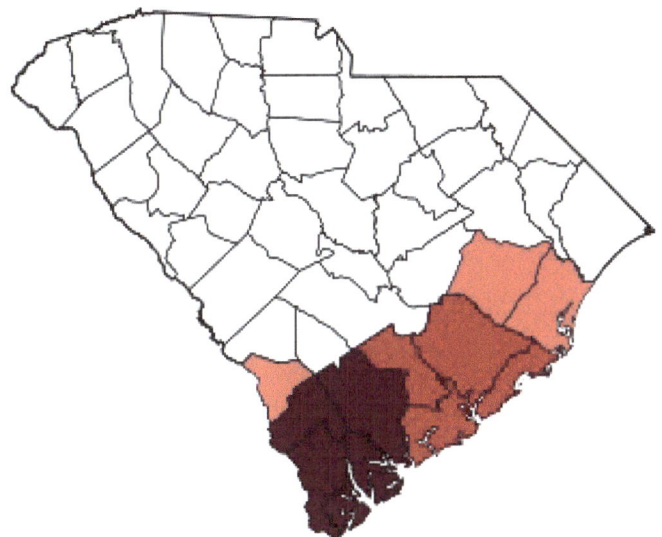

South Carolina – Carolina de Sur

Low Country

Pais bajo

The Lowcountry is the geographical and cultural region of the South Carolina coast including the Sea Islands. The Lowcountry and Sea Islands were once known for slavery- based wealth in rice and indigo. These plants thrived in the subtropical area of the Sea Islands. The geography of the Lowcountry is below the Sandhills of South Carolina. (Wikipedia> wiki>Lowcountry

The Sea Islands off the South Carolina Coast are Edisto, Lady, Wadmalaw, Morris, Callawassie, Port Royal, Bear, Folly, Morgan, Deewee, and James (Wikipedia>wiki> Sea Islands). The first people to live on the Sea Islands were the Native Americans of the Creek and Guale tribe (Sea Islands, United States/Britannica.com)

The Sea Islands also have a Georgia coastline. The islands of Georgia are Jekyll, Little St John, St Simons, Kiawah, Amelia, Cumberland, Tybee, St Helena, Hilton Head, Sapelo, Brunswick, Hird, Hutchison, and Bird. (Wikipedia>wiki>Sea_Islands)

The Sea Islands of North Carolina are Cedar, Emerald Isle, Harker, Hatteras, Knotts, Pleasure, Masonboro, Oak and, Ocracoke.

Sea Islands, Plantations, and Slavery were the unholy trio. Fortunes were made on the skilled forced labor -slaves. Hofwyl-Broadfield once boasted over 7000 acres of rice worked by more than 350 slaves from West Africa. The West African slave was imported for the skill sets concerning the tedious process of growing rice and rice production. West African slaves (rice and indigo agricultural skills) commanded a higher price value in the slave auctions

The Sea Islands were a similar climate and geography of West Africa including mosquitos, snakes, malaria, heat, and marshes. Life on the Sea Islands were hurricanes, ricebird invasions, insects, and swamp-marshland challenges. Many of the rice plantations were on the Sea Islands. The Plantation owners left a representative on the island, the slaves were isolated to the island. This was the beginning of the Gullah culture. (https://www.goldenisles.com/golden-isles/african-american -heritage) There is a difference between Gullah and Geechee. "Although the islands along the southeastern U.S. coast harbor the same collective of West African, the name Gullah has come to be the accepted name of the islanders in South Carolina, while Geechee refers to islanders of Georgia (https//www.georgiaencyclopedia.org/article/Gullah/Geechee.

"The West African slaves were the prime movers in the earliest days of rice cultivation in South Carolina. Rice was responsible for the area's rise to prominence in the colonial era." (Coclanis. Peter, A, Rice, www, scencyclopedia.org/sce/entries/rice/

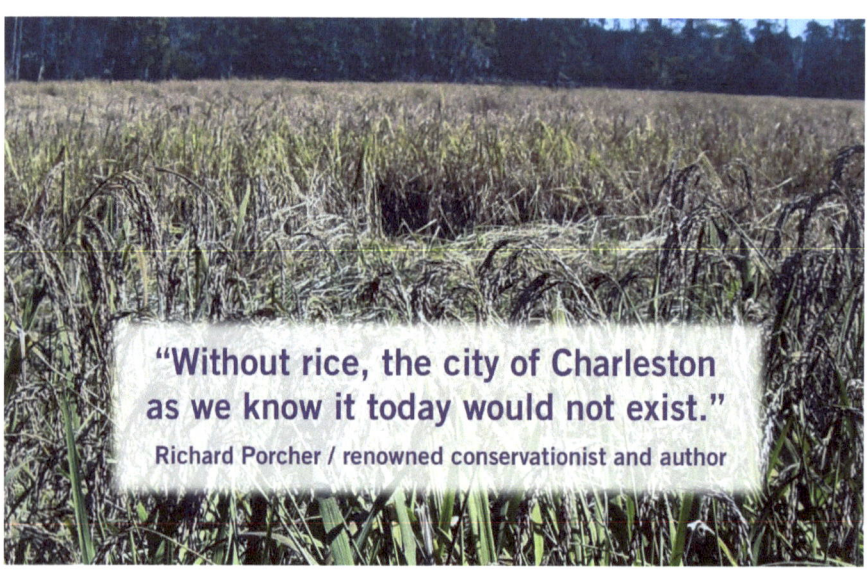

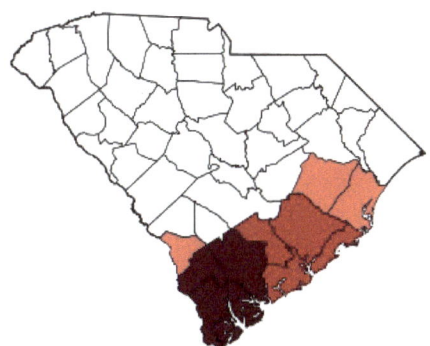

Carolina del Sur

Pais Bajo

El pais bajo es la region geografica y cultura de la costa de Carolina del Sur, incluidias las islas de Mar. Esta area Tambien era conocida por la esclavitud a base de arriz e indigo. La islas del mar extienden Carolina del Norte hasta Floridia.

La islats del mar tenian un clima similar al de Africa occidental y central. La islas tenian serpientes, pantanos, insectos, mosquitos, calor extremo, huracanes, aves de arroz, y malaria. Las islas eran perfecta para la produccion de arroz e indigo. (Wikipedia<wiki<Lowcountry)

"Los esclavos de Africa occidental fueron las principals motores de los primeros dias de cultivo de arroz en Carolina del Sur. Rice fue responsable del ascenso del area en la era colonial." (Colanis, Peter, A, Rice www.scencyclopedia.org/sce/entries/rice/)

"Sin arroz, la ciudad de Charleston tal como al conocemos hoy no existira" (Richard Porcher/reconcido conservacionista y autor)

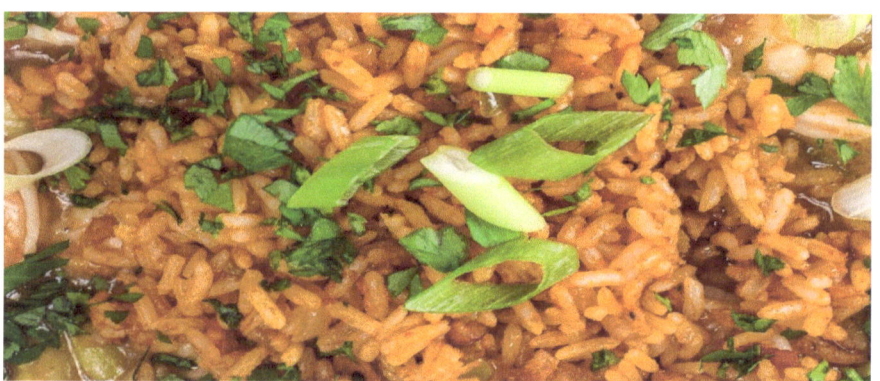

Arroz rojo Gullah con chorizo ahumado

Gullah Red Rice and Smoked Sausages

The short list of Lowcountry/Southern cuisine inspired by rice and the Gullah-Geechee people (descendants of West and Central African slave rice workers. The writer will address the evolution of the rice production slaves to the Gullah Geechee nation in a separate book. A guideline for Lowcountry and Seasonal cuisine is fresh, seasonal, and local ingredients. Some of the best Lowcountry and Southern cuisine is Old Charleston Style Shrimps and Grits, Robey Blue Crab, Deviled Eggs, Okra Rice, Teddy's Duck Gumbo, Stuffed Crabs Mushroom II, Tomato Pie, and Gullah Red Rice and Smoked Sausage(allrecipes>dish>lowcountry -southern.)

La breve lista de la cocina Gullah-Geechee inspirada en el Arroz son los camarones y semolas de Old Charleston, Cangrejos azules de Robey, Huevos rellenos, Arroz on okra, Teddy's Duck Gumbo, Camarones y semola de campo bajo, Pastel del tomate y Arroz rojo Gullah y salchichas ahumadas.(allrecipes>dish>lowcountry-southern)

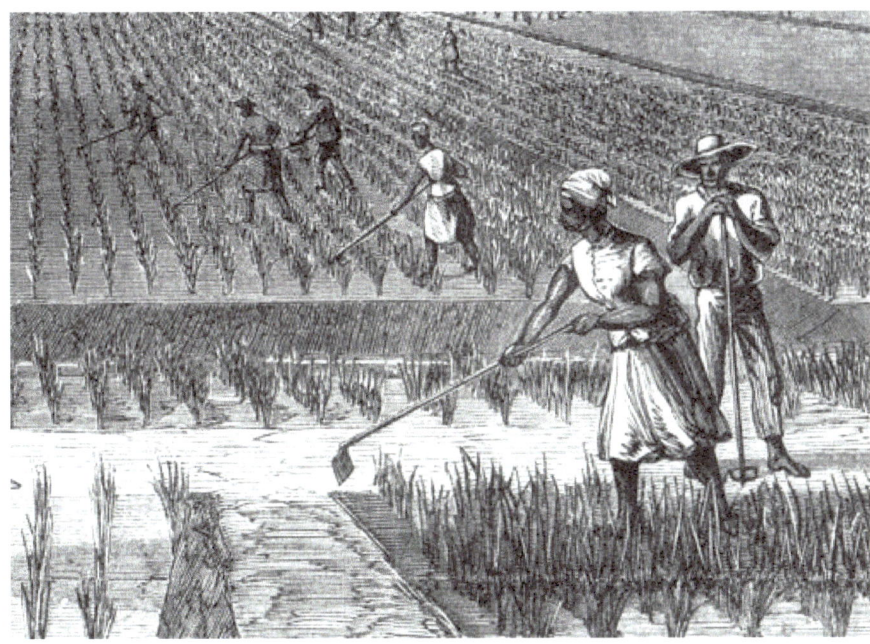

Rice Production in 18th Century

Oryza glaberrima commonly known as African Rice. It was domesticated and grown in West Africa. The rice was brought to America by enslaved West and Central African rice farmers. The plantation owners sought and purchased from areas known as the "Rice Coast" or "Windward Coast" The rice-growing areas of West and Central Africa are Senegal, Sierra Leone, Gold Coast and Liberia. (Wikipedia>wiki>Oryza glaberrima)

Rice was introduced to South Carolina in 1685. Captain John Thurber was sailing from Madagascar. He encountered a hurricane. He sought repairs in the Charleston Harbor. Captain Thurber gave Henry Woodward bag of rice. The love affair with rice began with this transaction. (Rice, Peter A. Colanis, South Carolina Encyclopedia, (https://www.scencyclopedia.org/see/entries/rice)

There is a special link between the Gullah and Sierrra Leone people. During the 1700 (18th century) the South Carolina and Georgia colonists discovered rice would grow well on the coast and Sea Islands. The South Carolina and Georgia colonists did not have the skill sets for rice production. There are specific skill sets for irrigation, planting, and harvesting. Rice is a difficult crop with a tedious process.(https://glc.yale.edu/gullah-rice-slavery-and -sierra Leone-american-connection.)

Africans from the Rice Coast were the largest group of slaves imported into South Carolina and Georgia during the 18th century. The plantation owners invested top dollars into Rice Coast African slaves. The skill set included cultivation of the rice. Cultivation entails seed preparation, land preparation, crop establishment, water management, nutrient management, crop health, management, harvesting and post-harvest(ricepedia.org>rice as-a -crop>how-rice -is grown) One of the most challenging elements is crop health. The rice plants have enemies such as rodents, insects, viruses, diseases and weeds. The weeds were managed by hand weeding and water/land management(https://glc.yale.edu/gullah-rice-slavery and -sierra-leone-american-connection)

Rice production was not merely unhealthy, but lethal. One 18th century writer wrote:

"if a work could be imagined peculiarly unwholesome and even fatal to health, it must be that of the standing like the negroes, ankle and mid-leg deep in water which floats an ouzy mud, and exposed all the while to a burning sun which makes the air they breathe hotter than human blood.("Rice and Slavery in America" Slavery in America Organization, Archived from original on January 1. 2007, Retrieved 24 June 2013)

South Carolina was the leading North American producer for almost two centuries from the late 1600s until the 1880s.(www.scencyclopedia.org/entries/rice)." The rice forged the plantation culture of South Carolina, Georgia, and North Carolina fueling both their economies and their cuisine. (Southern and Lowcountry). The ugly side, of course that the great wealth, it produced for its grower -and the city of Charleston itself- was built on the tortured backs of slaves" – Keith Pandolfi

The Civil War began the decline for rice as a cash crop for South Carolina. Asian rice had cheaper production costs and undermined the market share. The decline of the profitability of rice was also impacted by war time, destruction of infrastructure, emancipation of labor force, and postbellum transformation of agriculture. The Rice plantations on Sea Island could not use machinery in their agricultural mix. The marsh and swamp areas could not support the weight of heavy machinery. Natural disasters such as hurricanes during the years of 1893 to 1906 created further damage to decaying infrastructure. In the year 1919, the glory days of rice was gone.

The early 21st century cash generation source was based upon beach resorts, tourism and golf courses. (Rice, Peter A Colanis, South Carolina Encyclopedia (https://www.scencyclopedia.org/sec/entries/rice)

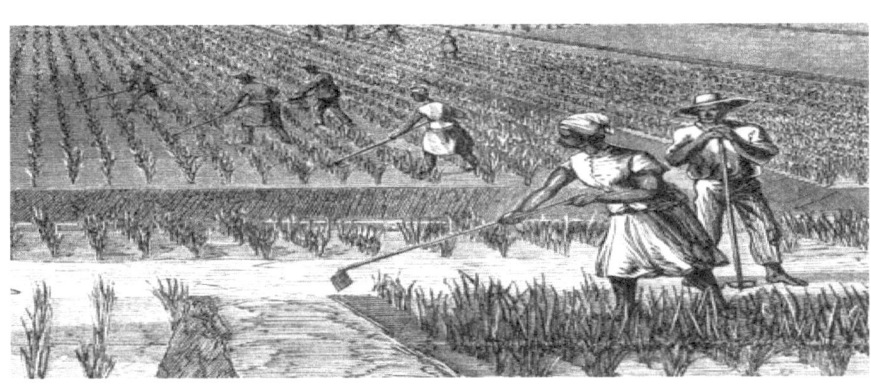

Produccion de arroz en el siglo XVIII

Orzy glaberrina se conoce comunmente como arroz africano. Fue domesticado a lo largo de las costa de arroz de Africa. Las semillas de arroz y las habilidades de produccion fueron traidas a America por escalvos africanos occidentales y centrales. (Wikipedia>wiki> Orzy glaberrina)

Los propietarios de plantaciones estsdounidenses invirtieron y compraron africanos de la costa del arroz. Esta personas tenian las habilidades de produccion de arroz. Tenian riego, sembra y cosecha. La produccion arroz es tediosa. Las plantas de arroz tienen enemigos como serpientes, roedores, virus, enfermedades, y malezas. Un escritor del siglo XVIII escribe "La produccion de arroz no solo fue insalubre sino lethal" (Rice and Slavery, "Slavery in America Organization, Retrieved 24 June 2013)

"El arroz forjo la cultura de las plantaciones…alimentando sus economias. El lado feo es las gran riqueza que produjo y la ciudad de Charleston en si, fue construida sobre las espaldas de los esclavos" (Kevin Pandolfi)

La Guerra Civil comenzo el declive del arroz como cultivo comercial para Carolina del Sur. El arroz asiatico tuvo costos de produccion mas bajos y una cuota de Mercado socavada.

La disminucion de la rentabilidad del arroz se vio affectada por el tiempo de Guerra, la destruccion de la infraestructura, la enamicipacion de la fuerza laboral y tranformacion de la agricultura despues de las Guerra. La plantaciones de arroz en las islas del Mar no podian usar maquinaria en la mezcla Agricola. Los hunedales, pantanos y pantano no podian soportar el peso de la maquinaria pesada.

Los desastres naturales como las huracanes durante los anos de 1893 a 1906 crearon mas danos en las infraestructura en descomposicion. El ano 1919, los dias de Gloria del arroz se hablan ido

La fuente de generacion de efectivo de principios del siglo XXI se baso en resorts de playa, golf y turismo (Rice, Peter A. Colanis, South Carolina Encyclopedia, https://www.scencyclopedia.org/see/entries/rice)

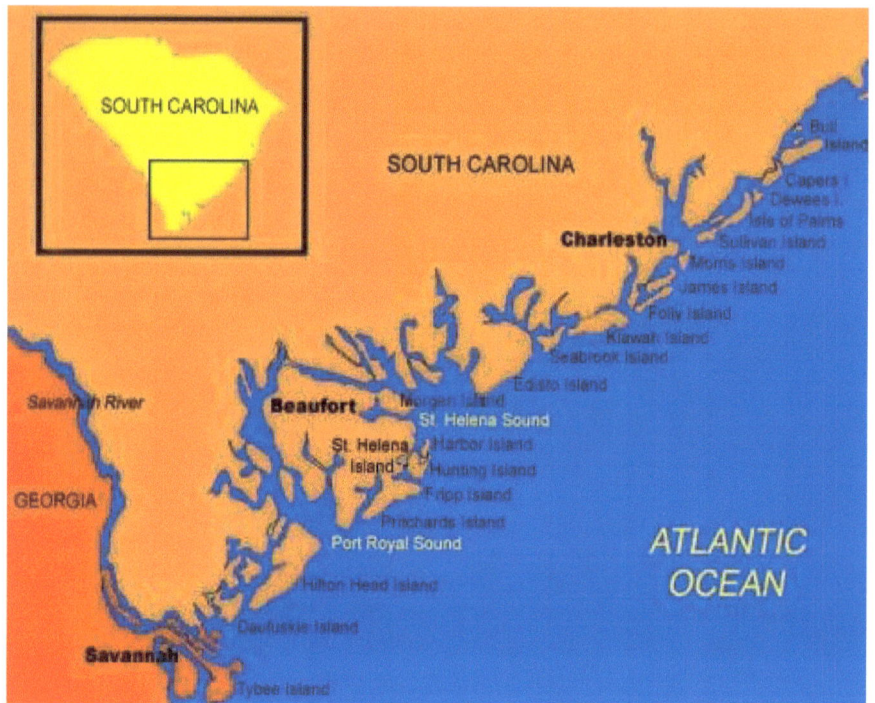

Sea Islands -Geographical area of Gullah-Geechee Nation

Islas del Mar – area geografica de la nacion Gullah Geechee

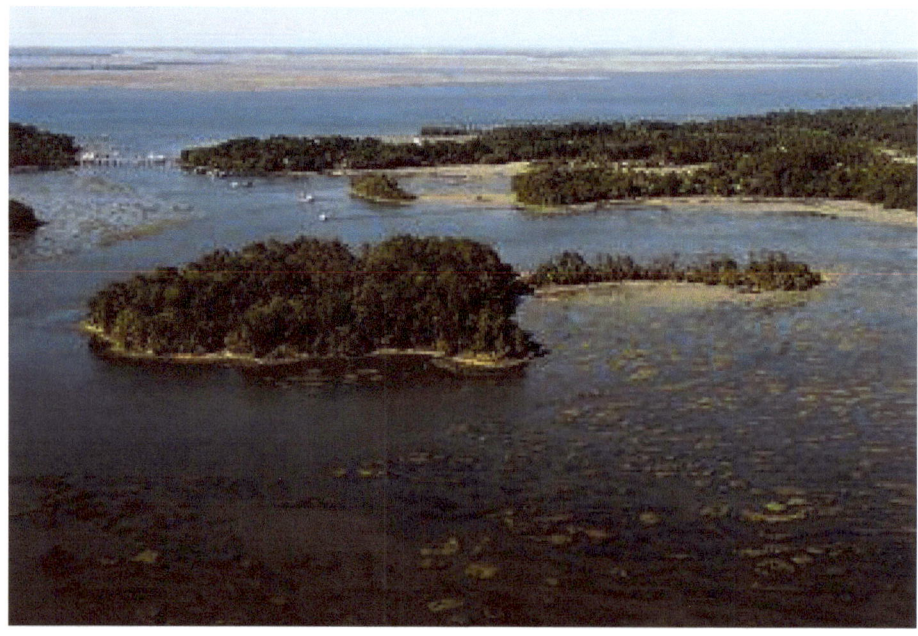

Sea Islands – Islas del Mar

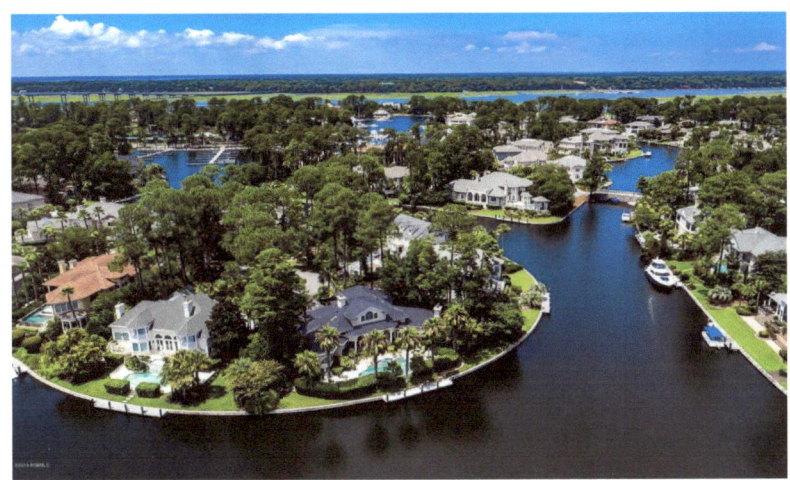

Hilton Head Island, South Carolina -Isla de Hilton Head, Carolina del Sur

Sea Island Stakeholders/Partes Interesada de la isla del mar

Tourism, Beach resorts, and golf courses are the primary options for the Sea Islands as economic profitability tools in the current century. Off-shore drilling is being brainstormed as an economic option. The stakeholders are the Gullah-Geechee Nations and the Beach Resort Developers. "The Sea Islands off the coast of South Carolina, Georgia, and Florida, also known as the Lowcountry has been home to the Gullah-Geechee community for the past 300 years... .and continue to live on the mainland and regions, "Sea Islands to this day" (Dominique T. Hazzard, https://repository.wellesley.edu/thesiscollection,/The-Gullah People-Justice, -and- the- land- on – Hilton Head Island: An - Historical- Perspective) Hilton Head Island is one of the popular tourism location in the Southeast.

El turismo es la principal Fuente de ingreso para Hilton Head Island. Gullah Geechee ha vivido en la isla durante 300 anos hasta la actualidad

Charles Fraser launched the Sea Pines Company in 1957. He purchased 5000 acres of the island for a high-class resort on the southern end of Hilton Head Island. The combination of the natural beauty (beaches) and private residential communities was a commercial success. The success of Tourism and private residentials communities had a negative impact upon the Gullah-Geechee community. There were decreased opportunities to fish, weave sweetgrass baskets, gardening, and increased focus on culture of servitude. "Numerous scholars have documented that rural black communities with higher rates of land ownership have a stronger sense of community and shared values "(Ibid) The Gullah-Geechee community also experienced reduced access to the land by legal interpretations of their property. There are fundamental legal and cultural differences between the Gullah Geechee and American concerning land ownership and heir property.

El tusismo tuve impacto negativo en la comunidad Gullah- Geechee. Hubo menos oportunidades para pescar, tejer cestas y para el jardin. El turismo aumento su enfoque en las cultura de la servidumbre. American y Gullah Geechee tienen diferentes conceptos culturales y legales sobre la proppiedad de la tierra. Las diferencias disminuyeron la propiedad de la tierra por el pueblo Gullah Geechee.

The Gullah-Geechee community is not a passive victim of history. In 2006, Congress passed the National Heritage Act, and designated the coastline from Wilmington, North Carolina to St John's County, Florida. This area is the Gullah Geechee Corridor. (https://gullahgeecheecorridor.org.)

Los Gullah Geechee no son victimas de la historia. El Congreso aprobo la ley Nacional de Hertiage en 2006. La Ley design lo costa desede Wilmington, Carolina del Norte hasta el condado de St John, Florida como el corridor Gullah Geechee

Nature is the stakeholder that commands the tourist, Gullah Geechee community and Beach resort developer's attention. The Sea Islands are fragile, environmental systems. The Sea Islands are not floating on the water. The islands are land masses or tops of volcanoes or sea mountains.

La naturaleza es la parte interesada que dirige los turistas, a la nacion Gullah Geechee y los desarrolladores de resorts de playas. Las islas del mar sori ecosistemas fragiles. Los ecosistemas cambian cada dia a traves de olas, Corrientes de marea, viento, aumento del nivel del mar, tormentas y mareas y mareas de tormenta. El excesivo Desarrollo de las islas del mar puede contribuir a la extinction de la vida marina, salvaje, y plantas. La belleza natural de las isla del mar puede convertirse en recuerdo. Te acuerdas……. en las islas del Mar.

The Sea Islands are constantly changing. Nature changes the islands by waves, current, tides, winds, sea level changes, and storms. The waves deposit and remove sediment from the ocean side of the island. Long shore currents create the waves hitting the island at an angle. The angle moves the sand from one side of the island to the other side. The Sea Island offshore currents move the sand from the northern side and re-deposit it on the southern end. Tides move the sediment into and fills the salt marshes. The sound sides of the Sea Island tend to build up as the ocean side erodes. The construction of building and creating vista views can require modification of waves and current flows. It could lead to accelerated ocean side erosion. The Beach Resort owner will eventually need to add more sand to refresh the receding beach. Beach refreshment is a temporary measure. The winds blow sediments from the beaches creating sand dunes. Sea level changes push the Sea Islands toward the mainland. Storms such as hurricanes create dramatic effects to the Sea Island. The storms create over washed areas, erodes the beaches and part of the islands.

Storm surges determine the impact on the storm on Sea Islands. The guidelines are based upon the U.S. Geological Survey (USGS):

1. Impact 1 Wave erosion confined to beach. The eroded sand will replenish in a few weeks to months.
2. Impact 2 Waves erode the dune and cause the dune to retreat. This is semi-permanent-permanent damage.
3. Impact 3 Water action exceeds the dune's elevation, destroys dune. Pushes sediment from dune landward (approximately 100m) creating overwash. The Sea Island is pushed landward.
4. Impact 4 Storm surge completely covers Sea Island, destroys dune system, pushes sediments landward (1 km). This is permanent damage to Sea Island or portions of it. (Craig Freudenrich, Ph.D., Science-howstuffworks.com: https://How Barrier Islands Work)

Balance is needed among cultural preservation, diversity, ecology, economic prosperity, wildlife preservation and nature, and innovation. Yin Yang, balance. When one teaches, two learn.

El equilibrio es necesario entre la preservacion cultural de la diversidad, la ecologia, la prosperidad economica, la preservacion de la vida silvestre, la naturaleza y la innovacion. Equilibrio Yin Yang. Cuando uno ensena, dos aprenden.

Copyright 2019 Lena Simmons

Online Purchase: Amazon.com Author Lena Simmons

Author Website: Amazon.com/ Lena Simmons Author

Facebook Page: Lena Simmons, Author

Twitter: Lena Simmons @Soulwriter2014

Publications

Summer of Cape Fear

El Verano de Cape Fear

Imagine Become

Freedom Hill

Canaan on Fire

Kairos

Woman Wisdom- Female Voice in the Bible

November Night

More than Male and Female

Haven't Lived for Nothing-Hymns, Hymns Makers

The Lioness Story

Women Wisdom – Bathsheba

Loving You- LGBTQ Youth

La Flor

Despues De Una Tarde de Lluvia – After an Afternoon Rain

Canaan – City on Fire

No More Babies

Women as Commodity

Humans Rights and Struggle

A Black Summer Night

Southern Sunflowers

Kwanza

Alma

Southern Sunflowers